EXIT *RIGHT*

Avoiding Detours and Roadblocks Along
the Baby Boomer Highway

Daniel P. Hazewski

8-14

ISBN: 1483978362
ISBN 13: 9781483978369

This book is dedicated to Buddy.
His spirit will ever ride the rails of the
Cape Cod Scenic Railroad.

"It is what it is..
It was what it was..
It will be, whatever it will be..."

Wherever you are, keep taking it one day at a time.

Author's Note

As with most things in life there are seldom perfect answers to the problems we may face. Exit Right is a compilation of issues faced over many years by clients and friends. I have changed names and sometimes circumstances in order to provide anonymity and better illustrate the many lessons found in this endeavor. It is my hope that these stories may provide you guidance as you travel your own road. It is my recommendation that you not travel this road alone. I encourage you to obtain specific and professional advice as you encounter the legal, tax, financial planning and life questions you will encounter in Exit Right.

To my clients and friends, thanks for taking me along for the ride! Drive safely and don't forget to *Exit Right!*

Dan Hazewski

Table of Contents

Every day I'd look in the mirror and see myself. It wasn't until I turned 80 that one day I saw an old lady.

83 year old woman to her grandson

Introduction

Whose face is that in my mirror? It looks like me but surely those lines and the graying hair must be a mistake. I don't see it but there it is. Others must see it as well.

Young men no longer need pose and posture, strut and puff. I am not a challenge to their masculinity. I'm too old to be competition. I have become invisible to younger women. I can only smile and take solace from September songs. I can joke that growing old is better than the alternative but the harsh reality is this: I am older. So are you.

That face in the mirror may not match the one we see in our heads but it is the one we carry around with us. And just as we have changed in appearance, so must we change how we plan for and see our lives. As baby boomers, we've been given a blessing and a curse. We are going to live longer, possibly too much longer, and if we don't plan well, too poorly.

I have spent the past 25 years working as a financial advisor. In the pages that follow, I hope to provide basic information to arm you, your spouse and your family for the coming challenges. This book is not going to tell you how to accumulate money, or offer clever techniques to maximize your income during retirement. While these are important issues, my purpose in writing is to help you understand the fundamental factors that determine whether you will grow old with dignity or difficulty. I want to make certain you don't look back some day and lament, "If I had only known!"

Fight it as we may, society and even our children will see us differently as we age. We may be questioned as to our competence and cognitive ability. We may become subject to rules and regulations that will force difficult decisions upon us. Society and the natural aging process conspire to deprive us of our ability to make our own financial decisions. In fact, the natural effects of aging deteriorate both our health and decision-making ability. If we live long enough, we may suffer diminished ability, become feeble and easily confused. For many, the capacity to make sound decisions will be taken away by the blight of dementia.

Ultimately, we enter into a phase of degeneration during which we cede control of our lives. This last, most unkind phase does not typically come upon us suddenly. It is a creeping disease during which we gradually lose mental capacity, physical health and reach an acceptance that someone else will be making decisions for us. Sadly, it often happens without our even knowing it.

At this point, the quality of our lives depends on whether we put a proper plan in place during our early years.

I would like to offer some encouragement. While we cannot stop the march of time and have little control over our mental and physical health, we can prepare to be in the best position possible. In the following pages you will find vignettes of real-life situations I have witnessed during my career. I hope by better understanding the obstacles we all encounter as we age, you can better prepare sooner rather than later how you wish to live during your later years.

And the autumn weather turns the leaves to gray, and I haven't got time for the waiting game.

September Song by Maxwell Anderson

Chapter 1
THE END

Joe was with a stranger when he finally died. *It wasn't what the family expected or intended. They had conducted the prerequisite vigils, following him from the hospital to the nursing home, back to the hospital and finally, back to the nursing home again.*

It was not that he persisted in living. Quite to the contrary, Joe had been at the point of dying for seven weeks. The emergency room physician who ordered him rehydrated didn't realize Joe was prepared to die. In fact, it was only by chance that Joe even needed to see the ER doctor. By the time he did, a series of strokes had rendered Joe little more than dead weight, evidenced by the fact that the hospital staff had to locate a hoist in order to lift him up for a CAT scan. Despite all this, poor Joe was, once again, being rudely brought back to a semi-conscious state of delirium and pain.

Comment

Joe's tragic example illustrates how vital it is to let your loved ones know your exact wishes should the most dire of circumstances occur. Traditional legal documents, such as Living Wills and Medical Proxies, may be the frontline of retaining dignity preceding your death. But equally important, your family and appointed legal agents must understand your final wishes. You must also choose someone with the fortitude and conviction to execute those wishes. The medical system is designed to prolong life. It does not discriminate as to the quality that life may represent, nor does it make judgments as to a patient's intentions.

Discussion

While any financial planner worth his salt will ask if you have the appropriate legal documents, the sad truth is that even with these documents, you may be treated differently than you would wish. Many people have the misconception that if their wishes are known, they will be followed, and if they are written, they must be executed. In my experience, few people have the necessary documents and fewer still have told their family the documents exist. Without knowledge of our wishes, how can we expect others to carry them out?

Medical crises can come upon us quickly. We all are aware of major warning signs: blurred vision, impaired speech, chest tightness and left arm numbness. Unfortunately, many other critical illnesses don't provide us the courtesy of such blatant announcement. When they do, we may ignore the warnings and instead suspect indigestion, muscle spasm or other non-lethal problem.

The fact is that we are all dying: Some faster than others, but all of us marching to the same final conclusion. While we might prefer immortality, most of us will end up injected into a medical system completely foreign to us, an environment where we are summarily deprived of our basic rights. Medical professionals will examine, prod, probe, inject and subject us to a plethora of procedures we would never agree to if we were not ill. Our humanity is stripped away as we cease being a person and are involuntarily assigned the status of patient.

At the end, it's the dichotomy between the medical system and human dignity. Although decisions about being kept alive through artificial means may seem relatively obvious at first, they become much more complicated when you finally arrive at impending death. Not only are you dealing with a system whose sole purpose is to keep you alive, you are probably unable to express yourself clearly or provide affirmation to those who will make decisions for you. When are those final decisions made? When is enough, enough? Does rehydrating a dying patient in order to prolong life a few additional weeks make sense or serve some public or spiritual higher good? Is it what Joe would have wished had he the ability to make his own decisions? If his living will calls for no feeding tubes, should the nursing staff be permitted to coax food into him if he becomes terminal? Does that fulfill his wishes?

Unfortunately, we live in a society so afraid of death that our laws forbid us the choice of when to die. We are subjugated by well-intended healthcare providers who have never been in a similar position and cannot fathom the idea that, at some point, death could be preferable to a nominal continued existence.

Deciding that it is time for your loved one to die is a heart-wrenching responsibility. When the decision has been made, even when conforming with the known wishes of that person, doubts may linger. Numerous and often unclear issues can complicate the equation: brain damage, severe incurable infirmity and disagreement among multiple decision makers can render the equation unsolvable.

How do you deny a life-prolonging procedure if a spark of hope still exists? What would the dying person do in your stead? The unknowns can mount and create uncertainty, indecision, family strife and distress that can influence the medical professionals as they try to address the needs of the patient. Given our litigious society, it's no wonder that legal counsel for medical facilities and their staffs has become a necessary part of the healthcare system.

While you cannot dictate all your wishes to fit every medical situation, you can and should have candid conversations with loved

ones regarding your feelings about artificially prolonging life and receiving medical treatment. It's not sufficient to simply state, "Don't keep me alive." There are many different situations that can arise and your loved ones will face difficult decisions. Your advanced directive documents must be clear to your designees. Your designees must understand what those documents allow them to do, as well as how those documents will be received by the medical community.

Traditionally, documents to be given to the medical staff designate several people, listed according to hierarchy, as the decision makers. Something as simple as understanding the meaning of a *and/or* or the phrase *if not available or competent* can be the difference between treatment and lack of treatment.

Your medical proxy and living will dictate how you wish to be treated at the most critical point of your life. The living will spells out the circumstances under which you do not wish to be kept alive. The medical proxy bestows decision-making authority on your trusted designee. As you might expect, these things are rarely a simple black and white issue but rather various shades of gray.

Suppose you say the following to your children:

"I do not wish to be kept alive by artificial means.

"I do not wish to live with diminished mental and physical ability.

Have you made your final wishes clear? Does your family know unequivocally what you want?

Consider Joe's case. It was clear to the family that he did not wish to be resuscitated only to linger in a diminished state of health. With the help of the doctor, the family finally agreed to deny Joe hydration through an IV or sustenance through a feeding tube.

Lying in a hospital bed, Joe was well beyond making any decisions at this point. His family decided to allow him to die.

As much as this difficult choice sounds like a merciful end to the story, the gray area now enters the picture. The dictate of a nursing home is different from that of Joe and his family. The nursing staff is skilled in sustaining life; they know how to coax sustenance into even an unwilling patient. Joe was given food and drink on a regular schedule. The meager nourishment he received was sufficient to keep Joe alive. His family agonized as they watched and waited, while his imminent death was postponed and his life prolonged. He was forced to linger for weeks, alive but not living. Was this the intended result of Joe's legal documents? Moreover, was this the desire of the family? What went wrong?

Lessons

1. **Talk to your family members** about your wishes for medical care, being kept alive by artificial means, and for internment and final services. Put your conclusions in writing and have several copies readily accessible.

2. **Your living will should specify exactly what you consider extraordinary or artificial means.** Don't shy away from discussing "What if?" scenarios with your family. The more they understand your wishes, the better they will feel when implementing them.

3. **The medical proxy will allow your agent to make medical decisions for you when you are unable.** It should clearly state the agent or agents and if there is an order of agents to be followed. The addition of phrases such as if not available or willing is important if you have indicated several agents in succession.

4. **Your family will be the best advocate of your wishes.** There's no assurance the medical practitioners you encounter will be made aware of your instructions; don't assume they will be. Without the direct participation of your agent/advocate, you may find yourself being treated in a manner contrary to your desires.

5. **In a medical crisis, expect confusion** and a lack of communication within the medical system as well as within your own family. It's vital that the family act in concert and that one family member convey those instructions.

6. **Medical insurance enters into the planning picture in many ways.** Generally, rehabilitation in a nursing home is covered while custodial care is not. Upon discharge from a hospital, you may be admitted to a facility for rehabilitation. While the cost of the care is covered, your wishes as a patient may be ignored.

7. **Once a patient is truly terminal, Hospice is often the best advocate.** Their services can be provided in any one of many places including nursing homes, the patient's home or their own facility.

"Don't cry because it's over. Smile because it happened!"

Dr. Seuss

Chapter 2

TIME FOR A CHANGE

It was midnight when Karen answered the call. It was her father, Frank. He had suffered a series of falls. The one tonight landed him in the hospital. Suspecting a stroke or heart attack, they wanted to keep him overnight for observation. Frank was the primary caregiver for Karen's mother, Margaret, and he knew his wife could not take care of herself without him. She might have another fall or perhaps another episode of leaving the teakettle to boil dry and ignite. With no options, Frank released himself from the hospital and drove home. Karen, the next nearest family member, was six hours away. Life would never be the same after this night.

Comment

Changing your life, while perhaps the right thing to do, may be difficult to accept. A dominant theme in our society is the struggle between aging parents and their adult children. When is the right time to recognize that something must change? How do you tell an aging parent they can no longer live alone? When is it time for an aging parent to accept they must give up driving and move closer to family? When is the right time to recognize that family support may not be enough, that skilled professional care may be needed? With the increase in our aging population, the need for retirement homes, assisted living, nursing homes and other facilities is outpacing the supply. Further complicating the planning process is that acceptance of this need for change typically occurs as the result of crisis. With limited availability of facilities, this acknowledgement often comes too late.

Discussion

I wish I had a crystal ball. Not to predict the stock market or which horse will come in first at the racetrack, but to better help my clients decide when it is time to make a change in their lives. Despite what the financial planning profession may profess, it is not a science, at least not in the sense that one can assemble facts, evaluate alternatives and reach identifiable conclusions. The only truly guaranteed thing about life is that it is not guaranteed. We can evaluate, quantify and analyze every nuance of the knowledge and wisdom of the past, but we cannot know for sure that we will wake up tomorrow morning. We cannot know what sinister demon may grow within us and raise its abhorrent head, spinning our lives out of control. One day things are fine and the world is good; the next day we are reminded that without our health, nothing else is of any real value.

It seems insidious to me that the same sense of "can do" and independence that propels our success during most of our life may become the force that wreaks so much turmoil in our elder years. While we can appreciate the forceful independence of an elder resisting the need for support, their blindness to reality often causes situations that only amplify the problem. **How do you provide care for a loved one separated by hundreds of miles?** Who takes care of mom and dad when they can no longer take care of themselves? I recall too many instances during a family meeting when the elder parents have closed their minds to the fact that they are in trouble. Driving down a street at a snail's pace, forgetting to take medication or forgetting which ones to take, burning the tea kettle, missing appointments, getting lost on the street where they live, the signals are clear if we only take time to look. Recognizing the signs can be the difference between a family handling crisis or chaos.

Our system of eldercare, while clearly imperfect is a system with rules. True it is somewhat different from community to community but essentially the steps to accessing care are the same. You do not wake up one morning and decide to go into an assisted living, nursing or retirement home. In each instance, two things must be present: qualification and availability. Qualification has two parts, financial and physical. Availability is a simple function of space versus people. The absence of any of these things leaves you out in the cold. Imagine the need to move Frank and Margaret closer to their family but with no place to go. Our older generation will be quick to say the kids should take them in. Perhaps they could but should they? An even bigger question is could they provide the care that is needed? What is the effect of an ill elder parent on the household of an adult child? I have yet to meet a client who wanted to be a burden to their children.

It's typical during a family meeting to see the parents smile at their adult children and tell them that they are perfectly fine living right where they are. It's also typical that something is wrong. Some event has triggered concern in the adult children, leading to the meeting. It may be as simple as seeing the home left unclean or in a state of disrepair, and the grass not mowed. It may be conversations during which mom tells the same stories she always tells but this time there's a suspicion she doesn't remember she has told them a million times before. Perhaps stacks of mail lay unopened or scattered asunder across the kitchen table. Whatever the signal, it must be heeded.

No one wishes to be uprooted and moved. Even more so, no one wishes to be categorized as entering the final stages of life. As nice as a retirement home may be, it is a homogenous gathering of people facing their end. As Frank said sarcastically when inspecting the apartment choices at his soon-to-be retirement home, "It's not important; it's only the last place we will live."

Painful as it may be to make the move, it is more painful not to do so. As our health deteriorates, we lose the ability to provide for ourselves. Rail at it as we may, once we are unable to provide for ourselves, we cannot exist independently.

Our dependence typically grows incrementally. It may start with the need for more frequent visits from family members. These visits may deteriorate from social to providing help around the home or with managing money and finances. Soon it may become evident that help is needed in handling prescriptions and doctor's visits. Often, without realizing it, family members are helping with all of the activities of daily living. As this dependence is accepted by the elder person it may become expected. Not only may it be expected, it may also be absolutely necessary. Without the help of someone else, it may be impossible for the elder person to safely live independently.

Crisis comes quickly and usually in multiples. A fine line exists between being able to live independently and the various stages of dependence brought about by declining physical and/or mental health. My vignette was a tragedy waiting to happen. Take two elderly people far away from family members, throw in debilitating illnesses, compound it with falls and fractures and then have one of them try to be the caregiver for the other. The result is a call in the middle of the night and multiple lives spinning out of control.

Lessons

1. **The decision by elders to move closer to family for support is typically the result of crisis** and too late for effective planning.

2. **When illness strikes, one elder spouse may attempt to be caregiver for the other.** Few people are physically, emotionally or educationally equipped to provide the needed care. In addition, this often results in declining health for the caregiver.

3. **Frequently, the eldercare giving spouse dies first,** leaving the surviving spouse (the patient) and his or her family scrambling to quickly put care in place. Often, this burden falls on the daughter living closest to the parent.

4. **An elder person's inability to remain living independently will exhibit numerous warning signs.** A professional should evaluate the situation if any doubt exists.

5. **Finding a place for mom or dad can be difficult.** Without prior planning, they may end up on a waiting list.

6. **Admission to a retirement home, assisted living or nursing home is not automatic.** The patient must qualify both physically and financially.

7. **The trauma that occurs when elder parents must be moved from their independent living affects the entire family.** Soon, everyone's day planner is filled with appointments and "TO DO's" for the parents. Meanwhile, family members try to somehow manage their own lives.

8. **There is no easy way to tell a parent they can no longer take care of themselves.** Be prepared for arguments and conflict from them, as well as from siblings.

"Old age takes away what we have inherited and gives us what we have earned."

Gerald Brenan

Chapter 3

THAT'S WHERE THE MONEY GOES!

It's not that Ted didn't understand, he did. He sat at the conference table with his checkbook. After numerous financial calculations, the planning was completed and he was being asked to give away two thirds of every dollar he and Grace owned. One third was to be a deposit for their new apartment in the retirement home; one third they were to give away to their children; the final third they would be allowed to keep. On paper everything should work. After a few years they should be able to qualify Grace for Medicaid.

Regardless of what the numbers said, Ted worried. He knew each dollar spent would never be replaced. His greatest, yet unspoken, fear was that he would not have enough, that he would last but his money would not. With a deep sigh and a shaky hand, he put pen to paper.

Comment

If you have done a good job of accumulating assets during your lifetime, the primary risk of outliving your income is not the allocation of your investments; it is your health. We now live in a society with the ability to sustain life, perhaps far longer than we would wish. The enormous cost of this medical care can not only wipe out a person's assets, it can also prematurely impoverish the spouse still living at home. Long term care and Medicaid planning have long presented questions with few good answers. While everyone, Congress included, recognizes the enormity of the current problem, no one has been willing to tackle the issue. Historically, the only answer has been to impoverish oneself and qualify for Medicaid.

Discussion

We live in a free society, that is, we are free to pursue life, liberty and happiness. Our founding fathers, however, declined to include healthcare as a fundamental freedom. Our system is one of pay as you go. Medical treatment is available if paid for directly from your pocket, or indirectly, through the provision of some type of health insurance. The one exception in the system is for the truly poor. If you are unfortunate enough to be truly poor you may qualify for medical treatment paid for by the Medicaid system. The qualification for Medicaid coverage is simple, have nothing. While I am oversimplifying the many regulations in this federally mandated, State run program, essentially if you have any money you don't qualify. You are on a pay your own bills, or "spend down" status. Additionally, regular health insurance, including Medicare does not pay for long term care.

Historically, most long term care planning, whether by professionals or individuals, involved giving everything away. I imagine that our "greatest" generation — one that watched their parents go through a depression and sacrificed 400,000 of their young men and women to a world war — found this concept abhorrent. The alternative, which is hard to imagine, was to spend everything you had. Those with little income and meager assets could qualify for Medicaid, where their expenses in nursing homes or for home healthcare would be paid through the social service system. Those with measurable assets of any kind could also qualify for Medicaid, but they would first have to level the playing field by spending their assets and giving up their income until they too had little. However, some people figured out they could beat the system. They divested virtually everything they owned by transferring their assets to a sympathetic child or a trust. So were their assets really gone?

Regulators quickly recognized transferring assets to families and trusts were an abuse of the system. They determined it was better to have people actually become poor as opposed to being poor on paper. They created rules that effectively preclude any strategy other than self-impoverishment in order to qualify for any type of long term care assistance. Congress inconceivably determined that it was legally and morally wrong to allow individuals who funded the system through their tax dollars to benefit from that system. They somehow reasoned that the system was designed to provide for those who could not afford to pay taxes. Their logic: put something in, get nothing out; put nothing in, get everything out.

The unintended victim of this irrational political mandate is often the husband or wife left at home to fend as best they can. Aside from the emotional trauma of losing a spouse to a nursing home, the resulting financial burden can be overwhelming. It's a classic sacrifice of giving up everything and putting yourself in jeopardy in order to provide for someone you love. Food and shelter are exchanged for medical care. By spending a life's savings in order to qualify for Medicaid, the "fortunate" spouse in the nursing home would be provided for, but the unfortunate spouse left with the household bills would have to depend on God and family. The trend in this illogical thinking is to make it more difficult for people with any level of financial means to access the Medicaid system without providing any alternatives that would leave a community spouse with any sort of financial independence. A lifetime of working, earning, saving and paying taxes may end in poverty.

We are all susceptible: we might lose all our assets, be forced to spend our income and become financially dependent rather than independent.

Lessons

1. **Medical insurance does not pay for nursing home and most home-based care.** Currently, Medicare Part A pays for 100 days of nursing care on a declining level, provided it is a skilled nursing facility and you are hospitalized for at least three days. It will not pay for custodial care.

2. **Home healthcare may be covered under Medicare Part A on a limited basis, with coverage restricted to skilled care prescribed by a physician.**

3. **Medicaid will pay for nursing home and some home healthcare for eligible applicants.** While the qualification differs from state to state, generally, couples can keep approximately $80,000, individuals only a few thousand. Currently, part of any income above a "maintenance" level for the community spouse must be contributed.

4. **Federal Medicaid programs are administered by the states, and often delegated to the county level.** Eligibility and other rules may vary from one municipality to another, but they typically follow the same overall guidelines.

5. **Giving away assets in order to qualify for Medicaid doesn't always work and could actually make you ineligible.** Ineligibility periods vary, depending on the size of the gift and the average

monthly cost of a nursing facility in the area. Currently, the ineligible period begins the date of application for Medicaid.

6. **Generally, you may own a vehicle, prepay a funeral, and keep your home yet still qualify for Medicaid.** Again, rules vary from place to place, and your home may be encumbered up to the amount of the Medicaid received. Keeping your home is dependent on someone still living in it.

7. **It's always a good idea to consult and engage an elder law attorney prior to making an application for Medicaid.** Ideally, do so long before needed in order to arrange your estate in the best manner practical for long term care planning.

8. **Long term care planning is always in flux as rules change and social service entities interpret them differently.**

"Electric communication will never be a substitute for the face of someone…who with their soul encourages another to be brave and true."

Charles Dickens

Chapter 4

THE BED RAIL

It was only a bed rail installed by Sara's daughter who was worried her aging mother would be injured. On the surface, not something that should fester disharmony among Sara's three children who took turns as their mother's caregiver. Sara was frequently falling out of bed so the daughter attached a child's bed railing as a precaution. She failed, however, to ask the other siblings before doing so, and it was now a source of conflict. Her two siblings argued via e-mail that Sara might still fall out of bed, taking the hard railing with her and causing even worse injury. While the quarrel may have been a control issue among the siblings, it was more likely an honest disagreement as to how to best provide for the safety of their mother. While communicating by e-mail may have been convenient, it eliminated the possibility of a dialogue. It was impersonal, a perfect medium to discuss their mother and the issues surrounding her care while retaining some emotional detachment. At a time when understanding was paramount, the lack of face to face conversation served to create dissention. The three children, though loving of each other and devoted to their mother, inadvertently chose an unreliable and easily misunderstood form of communication to make critical decisions about her future.

Comment

It's hard to measure the amount of stress thrust upon children whose aging parent is struggling through serious illness or incapacity. The parental roles are juxtaposed and confusion reigns as the children strive to assume and understand their new roles. There is little in life that prepares us to take charge of our parent's daily living activities. Trying to maintain some semblance of a normal life is virtually impossible while micromanaging your parent's care, health care providers and gaining consensus from your siblings. Life can become a day-to-day balancing act with stumbles waiting to occur. All of the familial feelings from childhood are rekindled — whether parent to child or sibling to sibling — and often inject themselves into conscious or subconscious decision making. Resentment, gratitude and a bevy of often-irrational feelings can overwhelm relationships and reason. Unchecked and without honest and frank dialogue, everyone's good intentions can eventually lead to separation rather than family unity.

Discussion

Managing the eldercare affairs of a parent is much like running a small business, except that family members make up the board of directors. For those who have never run a business or had to oversee scheduling, operations and procurement, the probability of failure is much greater. While failure in this case may not result in red ink and losses, it will result in family dissention and potentially poor decisions regarding the parent's wellbeing. Like a child caught in the middle of a divorce, conflicting opinions regarding the decisions for parents can drive wedges between family members. While unintentional, the ensuing emotional distress can overpower affection and common sense. Parental crisis is not a solitary disease; everyone in contact with the parent shares it. Those infected carry their own set of resulting symptoms.

Few of us are well equipped to provide eldercare although finances may seemingly force us to do so. We have no experience in the field and, as with most things in life, we learn by making mistakes. Unfortunately, in this particular field, our mistakes may be irreversible. Anyone trying to toilet an aging mother or transport an immobile father knows how difficult that can be. Without the proper training, we are more likely to injure them or ourselves than complete the task. Moreover, we need to ask if this is the role we want to take and one that our parents would wish us to assume. Do we really want our last memories of our parents to be that of changing their diapers? Would we wish this for our children when our turn to age and lose capacity occurs? While our guilt or sense of responsibility may drive us to overly intercede in the care giving, is it really in the best interest of everyone?

To successfully care for an aging, infirmed parent, we must honestly assess the roles we can play and how much we wish to give. Where does our oversight of care giving cross the line from manager to provider? Experience tells us that we can only react to the best of our ability and life experience. The emotionally detached daughter may or may not suddenly grow a desire to jump in with both feet and provide for her parents. Children who perceive themselves as unloved and neglected will likely have a very different reaction than those feeling the opposite. Growing up, the alpha sibling may find himself continually disagreeing with his brothers as they seek to exert their own adult dominance. Naturally, all of the undercurrents swirling among the adult children eventually will rise to the surface. Recognizing them for the divisiveness they create is essential to achieving the goal at hand — the proper care of the parent in crisis. Failure to recognize and cope with these disturbances will only lead to increasing disharmony to the detriment of all.

There are often many possible solutions to a given problem. It is also true that our decision as to which solution we see as best will be the result of our lifetime of personal experiences and feelings. We cannot help but bring our ingrained preferences and prejudices into our decision making process. As ignoring our own convictions is unlikely, the result we chose may appear the correct one to us but not to others involved or even the parents we are trying to help. It is important to remember differences of opinion will occur and exploring all of them will usually lead to the best answer.

The importance of a professional care co-coordinator cannot be overstated in dealing with parental crisis where multiple family members are involved. Someone who can effectively organize and supervise caregivers, continually evaluate the patient's physical and mental condition and provide direction for the family members is indispensable. As the eldercare industry reemerges as a critically important profession, there appears to be a shortage of qualified professional coordinators. While experienced in traditional care, many of those currently in the field are still learning and developing as new facilities, techniques and demands emerge from the growing numbers of newly elders. Clearly, the requirements of the baby boom generation will tax the ability to deliver care and counsel as never before.

In my vignette I describe a family trying to do the best they can as laypersons. Whether forced financially or chosen from some sense of loyalty or guilt, they are making caregiving decisions. Having no experience in dealing with an infirmed person who is able to roll out of bed, or perhaps being reluctant to impose too radical a change on their mother, the result is less than satisfactory to everyone. The conflict started by the bed rail could have easily been avoided through a conversation with a nursing home professional. The bed was too high. Lower it or get another designed for the job.

Lessons

1. **It's inevitable that disagreements will occur among families struggling through a crisis.** Understanding that the stress of

the situation is the cause, rather than the actions of others, will go far in working through the disharmony.

2. **It's natural that all parties involved with care giving — whether providers or family members — will approach matters differently.** The expertise brought to the problem by each individual should be recognized. It's unlikely that a layperson's contribution will be as significant as those with actual professional experience.

3. **The skill and experience of caregivers varies widely.** The competence and degree of care displayed in their prior employment should help you evaluate them relative to the requirements of your specific situation.

4. **Caring for an elder parent will bring about childhood resurgences of thoughts, actions and emotions.** Without deep understanding of what is occurring, it's easy to fall into psychological traps that will inhibit your ability to deal with the situation at hand.

5. **As with most controversial matters or those potentially creating conflict, using a third party professional can be very helpful.** It's difficult to be objective in serious situations involving those whom we love.

6. **As the care giving for an elder parent takes its natural course to death, outside caregivers involved may seemingly become closer to the family.** While it's important not to dismiss their empathy and even love for the patient, remember that they are employees who will eventually leave while your family members will remain to complete your cycle of life.

"Healthy is merely the slowest possible rate at which one can die."

Samuel Johnson

Chapter 5
'TILL DEATH DO US PART!

Dave was almost brusque during our interview. A self-made man, he managed his own business and investment portfolios. He was good with numbers, and could tell me exactly how much income came from his preferred stock. He knew the exact cost of the nursing home for his wife $95,000 a year.

Ironically, his wife Ann and his mother lived in the same facility. Dave had to divide his time between the two women when he visited. He did his best to please both but often without success. Old age and infirmity tend to amplify some personality traits while suppressing others. In this case tolerance, understanding and selflessness seemed to have taken a back seat. God only knows the stress he was under when visiting the women. He wondered what would happen to him if his wife lived too long. At age 78, his physical and emotional stress was evident the day we first met. I concluded that unless something changed, outliving his spouse and mother might be a problem he would never have to face.

COMMENT

It's difficult to ponder the death of a loved one, even more so to wish for it. I cannot imagine what form such a prayer would take or the guilt that might emanate from the eventual death. Even if blessed with substantial amounts of money, it's doubtful that any but the very wealthy can cover the cost of prolonged long-term care. The system discriminates reversely. Those with financial means must pay until they have nothing left, and those without financial means receive the same care. On the whole, it's difficult to differentiate who's occupying a hospital bed…a rich person or a poor one.

DISCUSSION

Sometimes, statistics are easy to understand but hard to live with. Statistics tell us that a couple retiring at age 65 have a 50% chance that one of them will live to the age of 93. Unfortunately, they do not tell us which one will do the living and if they can actually afford to do so. The financial planning industry has found this new phenomena — living too long — to be the source of great interest and untold consternation. Professors with PhD's concentrate their wisdom on devising products and planning tools that calculate how best to position our assets to last a lifetime. They create complementary calculators to help determine how much we can afford to spend annually so as not to deplete our funds. The bottom line is that while the ability to understand the need to extend our assets exists, the ability to control our expenses does not.

In Dave's case, it's inevitable that his ability to support himself and his spouse will decrease annually at a progressive rate. Since the income provided by his assets is inadequate to pay all of the bills, he will have to spend principal. Every year, his income needs will become a larger piece of a smaller pie. The crossover point, where the assets will begin to vanish exponentially, is just a matter of mathematics. The time when all of his money is gone will arrive sooner, rather than later.

Dave's strategy for taking money distributions has been to maintain his principal while spending the income it produces. It is a classic strategy used for generations in order to maintain principal. It requires living within one's means. One's means being the amount of income generated from the investments, plus any direct income, such as social security and pensions. Dave's assets are primarily invested in preferred stocks and bonds that generate interest and dividends. He did a good job of sorting through the investment offerings and his income stream is above benchmark averages. For many of the couple's retirement years, things were fine. With just one set of expenses to pay, they could enjoy life together as it should be: travel, gifts, dinners out and a few luxuries. The onset of Ann's cancer turned out to be a precursor of many less deadly but more debilitating illnesses. Now, with a stomach full of tumors, loss of equilibrium, amputation from diabetes and the onset of dementia, he can no longer care for her even though he wishes he could. They now live apart, he at home and she in the nursing home.

Dave projects to run out of money in seven years, when he will be 85 and she 83. If he is lucky, one of them will have died before this occurs. If not, she will finally qualify for Medicaid. Dave, however, will be broke. If he is unlucky enough to be blessed with his mother's longevity, he has only poverty to look forward to, having spent over a million dollars for his wife's care and his support. On the positive side, someone else will finally start paying the medical bills.

As children we believe we are immortal. Sticks and stones may break our bones but we have no fear of death. As older adults, we grow more fearful, knowing that **the real danger is not dying, but in living too long.** Despite the increasing number of elders in our society, we have not made the fundamental changes needed to deal with the enormous costs of prolonging life. Moreover, we have developed into a society willing to mortgage the assets of those left behind. Extending life, whether lacking in quality or filled with pain and humiliation, is more valued than allowing those left behind to continue their existence with dignity and comfort.

Dave could have potentially avoided this outcome had he known the rules and his future. His story is important because, like most people, he had the misconception that he would not be affected by events like this. He believed if he did the right things, worked hard and saved, and attained a degree of affluence, he would be protected from the tragedy of forced impoverishment. Reality shows us that medical enhancements, treatment facilities, and care and living centers can and will prolong our natural and often overdue deaths. Of course, all this comes at a cost that none but the very rich can afford without falling into the cycle of the welfare system. We have traded the fruitful and productive years of those not ill but left behind in the community for the temporary extension of life for the dying.

If you have never gone through the situations I describe here, you may find my insinuations callous and perhaps even immoral. But if you have a spouse or child, given the choice, would you extend your own life at their expense? Furthermore, would you wish to continue living in pain and humiliation knowing every breath you took and every treatment you received would be at the expense of your loved ones left behind? Until we find the fountain of youth, life will continue to be finite. While our medical advances are laudable, I suggest we are often confusing life with living.

Neither Dave nor any of his professional advisors could anticipate a situation where as a man of substantial means, he would be forced to spend down assets in order to qualify for Medicaid. Had Dave even considered the possibility, he could have taken steps to protect his assets and, therefore both he and his family's financial stability. As it is, we all await the results of time and circumstance completely out of our control.

Lessons

1. **Bad things do happen to everyone!** We have little control over our health and our health continues to be our major source of risk as we age, both medically and financially.

2. **Generally, everyone in medical facilities and nursing homes receives the same treatment, regardless of financial means.**

3. **Income planning for retirement must now take health into consideration, one with the potential to consume assets.**

4. **Longevity has become one of the major risks in planning retirement income distributions.**

5. **You must protect the principal of the assets you take with you into retirement.** It's unlikely that you will be able to replace lost principal.

6. **Until such time as long-term care healthcare is provided for us, we must do everything possible to plan to pay for it ourselves.**

7. **Life choices presented to us are rarely fair.** Our current system of dealing with long-term care requires sacrifices from those left behind to provide for those who are shortly departing.

8. **The medical system is often at odds with patients' personal desires.**

9. **The current techniques for Medicaid planning must change as the Medicaid system itself changes.**

It appears few of us will be exempt from the financial risks brought on by aging. As new techniques are developed to extend life, there will be a greater chance of impoverishment.

"When your life is falling apart, there's always an emphasis to hold on: to him, to her, to it; to the way it was, to how you wanted it to be, to how you want it now."

Learn to Let Go
Daphne Rose Kingma

Chapter 6
LETTING GO AND LET GOD

How valuable is sleep? You won't really know until it eludes you night after night.

Being sleep deprived weakened Mac's once-sharp mind. He was befuddled and could no longer think clearly. Dealing with insurance all of his life, he was adept with the yellow pad. Each time he came to my office, he would be clutching a new set of figures. Columns of numbers representing his estimated income and expenses graced every page. Each meeting he had a different variation on the same theme, none of which had quantifiable answers. Financial projections produce only estimates and guesstimates. Investment performance projections are filled with disclaimers stating, "This is what happened but there is no guarantee it will ever happen again." No one, even those gazing into a crystal ball, can tell us what the future holds or the cost. The best we can do is to plan and let go, let God.

Comment

The questions born of financial distress have no perfect answers. Financial planning is often a tradeoff of one set of undesirable consequences for another, particularly when addressing life's significant issues. For example, to qualify for Medicaid you literally cannot control any assets. Finding that fine balance between three sets of needs — yours, an infirmed spouse and the remainder of the family — can be a dichotomy lacking a clear-cut solution. The first step in maintaining your sanity is to realize that you do not have control over the situation. The second is understanding that any planning you undertake is based on assumptions that probably won't hold true. Numbers on a yellow pad may be in permanent ink but they are better written in pencil.

Discussion

To find the answer to most financial questions, you must understand the problem, recognize all the parameters that may affect it, sort through the available alternatives and finally, choose the course of action that makes the most sense. Unfortunately, the rules affecting long term care planning are often at odds with this strategy. It's apparent that pursuing a logical course of action — trying to preserve assets you have accumulated throughout a lifetime — may create another risk of loss. Selling things in order to "spend down" your assets to qualify for Medicaid may trigger income or capital gains taxes, or even a gift tax. Without getting into a discussion about the ethics of trying to save what you have, the choices bring into play taxes that normally would be avoided.

The most difficult aspect of financial planning may be the search for the perfect answer. It may stem from a client's doggedness or from a planner who feels guilt or remorse for not being able to provide the perfect answer. Life does not present us with solutions for every problem; it doesn't even guarantee us a fair break. We must accept the fact that all we can do is strive for the best possible solutions in an unknown and changing environment. While the planning industry has developed many sophisticated programs for cash flow analysis, retirement, investment growth and goal solving, it can't tell us when someone will become ill or die. It can't forewarn us that a spouse will lose a limb to diabetes, or that we may have our life shortened by cancer, cardiac or stroke.

Despite the best Monte Carlo simulations, planners cannot predict a terrorist attack that will send the value of our investments plummeting. Planning and reality are usually two different things, and projections are only as good as the moment and circumstances in which they were created. We cannot analyze away the unknown; we can only do the best we can and live each day as well as possible.

The yellow pad I describe above represents a complicated set of issues. For example, in order to qualify a spouse for Medicaid a couple may keep a small amount of assets, currently around $85,000 in most states. The couple may also keep their home as long as someone continues to live in it. At the same time, giving away assets will disqualify the couple from Medicaid for a certain period. How long is computed from a formula in which the amount of the gift is divided by the average cost of a nursing home in the area. If the monthly Medicaid cost in the area is $10,000 and the couple gives away $100,000, the period is ten months. This 'ineligibility' period begins the day they apply for Medicaid.

When applying for Medicaid, you must disclose your finances for a period of time prior to the application. This "look back" period is currently five years. If, as in the paragraph above, you have given away $100,000, you will not be eligible to receive Medicaid benefits until ten months after the date of the application. Common sense tells you to keep enough money to pay your own way for ten months until, under current rules, Medicaid starts to pick up the bills.

Using gifting, the "look back" period and the period of ineligibility caused by the gifting, it's possible to come up with numerous combinations to help qualify for Medicaid. Theoretically, you could give away everything you own except your house, wait five years, and then qualify for Medicaid, even though a Trust or your children now own your substantial assets. The dilemma, of course, is to determine how much to give away and how much to keep. This consideration is further complicated by your health. If you need long term care during this waiting period, who pays the bills? Here's an even bigger issue: what if you never need help? You have given everything away for no reason.

At this point, your eyes may be glazing over. The Catch 22 of eldercare planning is that one method of preserving assets is to give them away. However, while giving them away you must retain enough to sustain yourself for a very long time. Furthermore, the rules to qualify for Medicaid will change. What might make sense today may be totally irrelevant tomorrow.

Mac's problem, illustrated on his yellow pad, is not just trying to qualify under Medicaid rules; it also includes income taxes and capital gains. Like all of us, the assets he owns are treated differently for tax purposes. When he sells them, some will generate ordinary income, some capital gains; others may trigger little or no tax at all. Poor Mac is stuck. He needs enough money to pay the nursing home bills, must spend down his assets to qualify his spouse for Medicaid and simultaneously know which investments to sell.

While Mac loses sleep overanalyzing the numbers, the irony remains that he is fortunate to have adequate assets. His dilemma is balancing the financial support of his wife with the possibility that she may outlive them both. A reasonable person might conclude Mac has more than adequate resources to accomplish whatever he wants in life. However, the unreasonable cost of long term care tells us otherwise. Except for the very wealthy, we all risk the possibility of outliving our assets due to the cost of eldercare. Because we cannot know what the future will bring, overanalyzing the numbers will not result in better planning...only less sleep. While it's hard to accept there are no perfect solutions, it's best to know the truth. Our best-laid plans may not work as intended. Accepting that things may change and reacting as those changes unfold may be the best activity we can pursue. Certainly, acceptance will at least allow us to sleep better at night.

Lessons

1. **Financial planning is not an exact science.** Your assumptions are as likely to be incorrect as correct.

2. **The broader concept of long term care planning is more important than the minor details.** Medicaid can pay for long term care for those who qualify.

3. **Qualifying for Medicaid involves examination of assets, income and any gifting you have done.**

4. **The "look back" period is the amount of time you must disclose your financial records when trying to qualify for Medicaid.**

5. **Gifting during a "look back" period will make you ineligible for Medicaid for a period of time.** The disqualification period depends on the size of the gift and starts the date you apply.

6. **Medicaid is a Federal program run by the States and usually administered by local Social Service agencies.** The interpretation of the rules may vary from state to state and even county to county.

7. **Medicaid planning often involves your health, assets, expenses and how much to gift or keep.**

8. **Different assets are taxed at different rates that can fluctuate.** IRA's are ordinary income, while other investments may create capital gains.

9. **The only guarantee in Medicaid planning is that the rules will change.**

"You have to learn to steal from yourself in order to survive!"

Richard A. Leonelli

Chapter 7

WHO'S ON FIRST?

My wife pointed out to me that Nick was always distracted, which is why it was so difficult for us to communicate. I had his portfolio holdings displayed on the widescreen monitor in our office but I couldn't get him to concentrate on the important issue we were discussing. I pointed out that his preferred stock, particularly in the real estate sector, was getting badly beaten up by the financial crisis and he needed to liquidate. He insisted the dividends were good and wanted to keep the stock. We both knew he would have to sell something. He needed cash to cover his wife's $11,000 monthly nursing home bill but he only had $2,000 in his cash account. Obviously, we had to sell something to generate the needed cash, but what to sell? The stocks that were losing so much value or something else that had fared better? The irony is that it really didn't matter. The plan was to use up all the money in five years anyway. How could losing money in the stock market be a good thing? Somehow the conversation sounded like an Abbot and Costello skit, "Who's on First?"

Comment

The subtleties of a situation sometimes elude us. All our life, we are told we should never spend our principal. We know that investments combining higher dividends or interest rates with less risk are a better choice than those that do not. We invest and accumulate a nest egg to provide for our lifetime. But there are times when the best course of action is to ignore common sense and do the opposite. Is it illogical to worry about the performance of an investment we have to deplete? Is there any sense to keeping the investments that are doing well and selling those that are not if the end result must be to liquidate them all anyway?

Discussion

You've learned that qualifying for Medicaid involves two tests: the look back period and the period of ineligibility. The look back test involves opening up your records from the date you apply for Medicaid and doing a show and tell. You must reveal all of your financial records for the previous five years. If you have made any gifts during that time, you are ineligible for Medicaid for a specific number of months, derived from a simple formula: Divide the amount of the gift by the average nursing home cost, as determined by the local social services for that area. The result is the period of ineligibility and it begins at the date you apply. If you had given away $200,000 during the look back period and the nursing home cost is $5,000 monthly, you would be ineligible for Medicaid assistance for 40 months from the date of the application. You would be obliged to pay your own way for 40 months before receiving any assistance from Medicaid.

If you are applying for Medicaid and have assets you must spend or gift to qualify, timing of the gifts is essential. Since giving away funds makes you ineligible, you must carefully plan how much to give away and how much to keep. Why? Because if you become ill, someone will have to pay the nursing home bills that Medicaid doesn't. Your gift, in order to qualify, has made you ineligible. If you give away too much, you won't have money to get you through the ineligibility period; if you keep too much, you will have to "spend down" your assets to the correct level.

Another point: the look back period is a moving target. Each gift you make triggers a new look back period from the date of that gift. Let's assume I planned to put myself in a position to qualify for Medicaid if needed. I could give away everything I own, wait five years and apply for Medicaid. Theoretically, I should qualify since all the gifts were made prior to the look back period and do not need to be disclosed. What if I make another gift two months from now? I will have stretched my look back period to five years and two months from the date of the first gift. If this seems confusing, try to remember that show and tell is for five years looking back and ineligibility is based on the amount of the gift from the date you apply for Medicaid.

So who's on first? In a normal world, you would be concerned about the performance of the investments in your portfolio. You would seek to maintain your principal and generate a reasonable rate of return. In the abnormal world of eldercare planning as described above, in order for the plan to work, your investments must be gone by the end of the look back period. Imagine looking at an investment and saying, "This is doing too well. If it continues like this, I'll have too much money at the end of the five-year period." Imagine looking at an investment that is losing value each year and thinking that it's doing what is necessary. Of course, you have the balancing act of being sure your funds last long enough to get past the look back period. If you run out of money, nobody is going to help.

In the vignette at the beginning of this chapter, the tragedy involves a nearly 80 year-old man who is trying to unlearn every financial tenet he believed in throughout his life. He is already distraught being separated from his wife of fifty years. He is afraid of what will happen to her and what will happen to him should they be unfortunate enough to live for an extended time. He had the intelligence to accumulate enough money to ensure he was never a burden to his children or society, but he must now cope with the realization that in order to survive, he must impoverish himself.

Suddenly, our conversation about what to keep or sell is irrelevant and inane. If we do too well, we will have too much money. If we do too poorly, we will not have enough. If something does too well we should sell it. If something is doing poorly we should keep it. What if the things that are doing poorly improve in the future? Should we not take the chance they may rebound and sell them now while they are low? What if the things doing well continue to do well? Should we sell them before they have the chance to grow too large? Why don't we just turn everything to cash and spend as much as we can? If we do that, will the money last long enough? If who's on first, what's on second? I don't know!

Lessons

1. **Medicaid is a federal program administered by the states and local communities.**

2. **To qualify for Medicaid, you must spend down assets to a minimal level set by your state.** As a rule, you are allowed to keep less than $5,000; a married couple can keep up to $90,000 in some states.

3. **To qualify for Medicaid, assets are often gifted to family or a Trust.** Assets not given away are spent for care and maintenance.

4. **The look back period is the period of time from the date of Medicaid application backwards; you must disclose your finances, including any gifts.** It is currently five years but can change.

5. **The amount of any gifts made during the look back period determines the number of months the grantor is ineligible for Medicaid.**

6. **The number of months of ineligibility is determined by dividing the size of the gift by an average monthly nursing home cost used by the local Medicaid-providing entity.**

7. **IRA accounts are difficult to use in planning as any gifting involves the recognition of ordinary income taxes upon completion.**

8. **IRA accounts are semi-exempt in some areas for those over the age of 59 1/2.** While you don't have to spend down the assets, you must turn it into an income stream to be used for your care.

9. **If Medicaid qualification is the prime financial objective, the portfolio performance of any assets retained becomes less important than successfully spending down the assets throughout the look back period.**

10. **Additional gifts made during a designated look back period will cause a new look back period to begin for the amount of the gifts.** If you continue to make gifts, you continue to extend the period of time before which you can become eligible for Medicaid.

11. **Some planning is more important than others.** It's essential to prioritize your financial objectives and not lose sight of what you are trying to accomplish. This is particularly difficult in circumstances where you are forced to act differently than you would normally.

12. **Discussions concerning Medicaid planning must be honest and open.** They will likely be uncomfortable for all parties. Planning professionals must be able to involve you in conversations you understand. Never lose sight of what you are trying to accomplish.

"Don't let aging get you down. It's too hard to get up!"

John Wagner

Chapter 8

SORTING THROUGH THE MESS

The appointment went differently than either of us expected. Our past meetings had always found Jonathon upbeat and at his best. A successful CEO, he was a problem solver, a man who could gather information from his advisors and make astute decisions. I asked him about his wife, Tara. His shoulders sunk and the brightness left his eyes. Tara had been in and out of hospice care three times in the past two years and barely clung to life. Meanwhile, Jonathon took over the household chores. He cleaned, cooked, scheduled, and drove, dressed, showered and toileted his wife. He even tried to make her favorite cake. Now he worried about what would happen when he could no longer take care of her. His greatest fear was that he would die first, leaving her alone. In an uncharacteristic outburst, he exclaimed how she never even thanked him. I said, "Jon, you're going to burn yourself out and be of no help to anyone." He sighed, "I am burned out Dan. I am!"

Comment

No one truly understands the eldercare system until they go through it. While attractive new retirement facilities are erected in anticipation of the aging baby boom generation, they are merely a temporary stop on the road to a place no one wishes to go yet everyone is headed. Healthy affluent people will always be welcome in facilities resembling country clubs more than retirement homes. But where do once-beautiful people go when their bodies betray them and they are no longer beautiful? When they are simply worn out or too damaged to function? Who do they turn to for guidance through the maze of agencies and facilities?

Discussion

Soon there will be more people retired than working, creating an enormous strain on an eldercare system already in trouble. Our parents were compliant. It was not their nature to complain or question authority. Doctors were always right; religious leaders spoke the word of God. But the next generation recognized doctors had clay feet and sin could be redefined to better fit the lifestyle du jour. They would question before accepting anything. The quagmire of elder health care needs questioning and improvement.

Whether the motivation is love, pride or lack of money, some try to provide for their spouse well past the point when the need for an outside caregiver is obvious. Sadly, their loving efforts can be to the detriment of both. It's difficult for us to accept advancing age, to see that we have become a different person. While we may be forced to accept that we are no longer as strong or vigorous, it's hard to accept we are no longer capable. How then do we acknowledge that we are no longer in control, that we need help?

Our transition to a nursing home is often a clear path   a default from hospital stay to rehabilitation center, usually within a nursing home. It's just a matter of which side of the facility we're living in rehab or long-term care. Once you're in long-term care, you are set for life, however short or long it may be. A larger problem occurs if you don't fit into the system. What if you have an illness but it does not require hospitalization, let alone rehabilitation? You are at home, progressing through the illness with a series of doctor visits and outpatient testing. As you progressively lose your independence, your spouse takes over responsibility for your daily care. Eventually, you become a couple with one elderly person trying to take care of another. The short visits from friends, family and the Home Health Care nurse are welcome but not a permanent respite. Gradually, the authorized healthcare visits are used up, friends drop by less frequently and family members, despite their guilt, resume their own lives. The situation deteriorates into a crisis, one the family fails to recognize in time.

So how do you find a caregiver? How do you pay that person? There is no standard answer because there are many ways to approach the problem. A myriad of public and private agencies exist to facilitate eldercare. Many more are emerging, hoping to benefit from the enormous financial potential. How do you sort through the alphabet of agencies to find the one that can actually help? How is that agency or person paid and by whom? Complicating matters are State and Federal regulations, as well as insurance company contractual language that define and restrict who is a qualified caregiver. If you intend to have the care paid for by Medicare or a private health insurance policy, you may be in for a surprise if you pick an agency or person who does not qualify.

Sometimes, eldercare situations fall outside the system. While agencies can provide caregivers, a subculture of independent caregivers also exists, people who insist on being paid under the table. These people may or may not be qualified to provide the type of care needed. If their last position was caring for someone now deceased, reliable references may not be available. Your first opportunity to evaluate their competence may be after they have been hired to care for your loved one.

It's also not unusual to find agency caregivers who would rather work directly for you since they get to keep all the money. In good conscience, can you pay a caregiver directly? Does that make you an employer? If so, do you need to report payroll tax? Do you need insurance? What is your responsibility if the caregiver is injured on the job? As an employer, are you responsible to pay overtime after 40 hours? Are you required to provide employees a break every four hours? How do you do so with a live-in caregiver? If around-the-clock care is required, how many caregivers do you need?

Another issue is sorting through who pays for what. Home healthcare costs can be enormous and the community spouse, the one not receiving care, is sensitive to what is covered and for how long. Unfortunately, Medicare does not pay for continuous home health care, much less nursing home care. Lacking insurance or additional sources of wealth, the cost can eventually deplete the patient's assets.

Currently, the cost of full time care averages between $250 and $400 a day, and can exceed $12,000 monthly, not including over-time. Nursing homes typically cost less but may not be the right choice.

The historic scenario of spending a lifetime working for the same company, retiring and dying five years later no longer holds true. Medical science has extended our lives but the eldercare in-dustry has not kept up with our housing needs. Surviving spouses do not wish to go live with the kids. Many elders are not ill enough to require a nursing home but require more help than can be found in assisted living facilities. As millions of baby boomers see their lives extended for decades, securing appropriate housing will become an even more critical issue.

Jon had adequate funds to provide for Tara. His dilemma was one of guilt related to her illness. He felt his obligation to his lifetime spouse was to do everything for her, keep her at home and make that home as normal as possible. He was exhausted trying to do it all perfectly. Little did he know that without outside help, he could be the first to die.

Lessons

1. **Caring for an elder spouse creates great stress, both physical and emotional.** The eldercare giver may be ill equipped to perform the necessary tasks and the immediate family reluctant to intervene, despite clear signals that things are too difficult for the caregiver.

2. **A professional should coordinate care.** The intricacies and relationships (or lack of) between various agencies can be overwhelming. Resources may be overlooked because the family is unaware they exist.

3. **The health insurance system — both Medicare and private health policies — provides rehabilitation following hospital stays but does not provide funds for custodial care.**

4. **Activities of daily living (ADL's) such as mobility, feeding, dressing, toileting and bathing, are used to determine health status for independent living. Their absence is often the triggering event for insurance payments.**

5. **The inability to perform ADL's must be certified by a medical professional.** If insurance is to pay for care, the caregiver must be medically qualified and often cannot be a family member.

6. **Several avenues exist for obtaining caregivers, including agencies, registered individuals and independents.**

7. **Hiring a self-employed individual can be problematic.** It can be argued that you have become the employer and if so, exposed to all the rules governing any employer.

8. **The skill level of caregivers must equal the level of care needed.**

9. **As a patient's health deteriorates, it may be necessary to move to a different facility offering the necessary care.**

10. **It's vital to determine the competency of both the facility and the individual caregiver.** Failure to do so can result in a forced change of one or both.

"Careful what you wish for,
Be careful what you do,
Even when you whisper,
Someone is listening to you."
Careful what you wish for

Jonatha Brooke

Chapter 9
WHO DO YOU TRUST?

When Carl came in for a short visit, he looked much better than he had in quite some time. "You know Dan, I've been out of touch for several months," he said. By out of touch, he really meant unable to cope following the death of his wife. He had been going through a semblance of living without actually participating and was now ready to reemerge into humanity.

Carl asked about the money he had previously gifted to his son. I reminded him about the trust his attorney had established in order to avoid the state inheritance tax. As trustee, his son was the only one who could actually direct transactions. Yes, the money once belonged to Carl but that made no difference under the law. Once gifted, his funds were gone and it would be illegal for me to acquiesce to any of his instructions. Simply put, the planning we had done avoided taxes, but also took away all of Carl's control. If he wanted money, he would have to ask his son.

Comment

There are many useful reasons for creating trusts, such as managing assets, to reduce or eliminate taxes or to provide for the welfare of minors or less competent individuals. Trusts can be an instrument to allow a business to continue after the owner's death. They can be as rigid or flexible as necessary. Revocable trusts include a set of rules designed to accomplish a specific goal or task. Irrevocable (non-revocable) trusts achieve the same objective but lack the flexibility to make changes. Obviously, if you are going to create a document that can never be changed, you should be absolutely certain you are doing the right thing. Think of an ir-revocable trust as entering into a contract longer than life. Who among us has never done something they wish they could undo?

Discussion

Unfortunately, much of our life and planning revolves around man-made rules and regulations that dictate what we can and can-not do. They control how we must legally act and, in many cases, who we are obligated to pay. In the area of income, gift and estate tax planning, we must understand the rules in order to minimize how much we must pay. Historically, the largest taxes are associ-ated with estate planning. As a result, it's become a major industry, with the prerequisite cadre of consultants who must be retained, employees who must paid and provided benefits, revenue that must be collected and redistributed by governments, and tomes of written documents and statutes. In my experience, the primary function of all of this documentation is to be so confusing as to in-sure the continuation of the system. You simply can't do it yourself.

The heart of the issue, as always, is money…your money and whether you get to keep it or contribute it to the general welfare. Estate planning is much like a childhood game in which you get to choose up sides. My team takes an attorney to help us understand the rules of the game; an accountant so we know how much we are playing for; a financial planner to provide coaching and make sure team members are talking to one other; and possibly a trust department or trustee to ensure everyone is playing fairly.

The other team has a small army of bureaucrats consisting of agents, attorneys, staffers, administrators and professional collec-tion people. And these aren't just local people. They come from all levels of government to make sure their team wins and you lose. After all, this is a big game! At stake are the jobs of all the players from both sides.

Now try to imagine a tax system so simple and fair that it has no need for rules, attorneys, accountants or bureaucrats. Think of the effect on the economy if we eliminated all of the jobs created by our system of taxation. It is essential that you ultimately lose because your money is needed to perpetuate the industry. Not only does the estate planning industry need your money, governments need your tax dollars in order to continue to function. The whole system of goods and services we have all come to rely on cannot exist without the spoils of our misfortune — your dollars.

Trusts, both revocable and irrevocable, have become the favored instrument of estate planning. Think of a trust the same as a business structure. A trust can be an individual doing business as something else. All that has happened is that you are identifying yourself with a different name. It can also be an entity with its own life — think of a corporation where you and the trust are treated legally as separate entities. The trust even has its own tax ID number and files its own tax returns.

With a revocable trust, we create a business to do specific things that are spelled out in the document or business plan. It can hold property, buy and sell things, make gifts, invest, spend and save just like an individual, because it is we who are doing it. Since we still can change our minds about everything at any time, all that has happened is that we have dressed ourselves differently, trying to disguise ourselves. Our opponents in the tax collection tax game can see through the new clothing, recognize us and treat us accordingly. This can lead to misfortune if we incorrectly believe that the revocable trust actually protects anything. It does not.

Since you can change your mind about a revocable trust at any time, put things into it or take them out to benefit yourself, direct how things occur and what the trustee can and can't do, then everything within the trust really belongs to you. Sure, the legal owner may be the trust but when it comes time to tally up the tax bill, guess what? It doesn't pass the smell test. You may have gifted things away to the trust on paper, but they really didn't go far. Since you retain control, everything in the trust is still yours for tax purposes. It will not save your assets from estate or inheritance tax, nor will it preserve your assets in Medicaid spending plans.

While it doesn't provide any benefits when it comes to big-ticket items, there are some good uses for a revocable trust. It is private, avoids probate and can facilitate the use of professionals in situations where they are needed. It can also become irrevocable should the person forming the trust die.

The irrevocable trust represents the corporate example I previously mentioned. It functions independently of you as the donor, and is its own entity. Yes, I said donor because in an irrevocable trust, you make a completed gift — money, property or investment portfolios are actually given away. Instead of you owning and controlling these assets, the trust owns everything and the trustee manages them for the benefit of the trust beneficiaries. **The important point here is that the things given away are truly no longer yours.** It's a done deal and any attempt or special language allowing you to control the trust assets brings them right back into your estate where they are subject to taxes and creditors, including the Medicaid system. If you have gone through the effort and expense of forming trusts, your intention would certainly not be to make them irrelevant.

The one thing we know for certain is that nothing ever remains the same. Just as we change from infant to adult and sometimes back to infant, the system of rules and regulations we must live under changes with each new political administration or Supreme Court decision. What was good planning in 1980 became irrelevant in the year 2000. Don't despair. It may come back to pertinence at any time, depending upon a congressional vote or presidential veto.

How then do you put a plan permanently in place that will do what was intended when needed? Imagine creating something you can never change. As time passes by, the rules change, and now the thing you created so carefully may be all wrong. As the saying goes, "Be careful what you wish for; it might come true."

In Carl's case, his trusts were made with good intentions to preserve as much as possible from estate and inheritance taxes. This was accomplished, not because of the planning and trusts, but because the rules changed. The taxes would not have applied in any case. In the meantime, Carl gave away most of what he owned. His son was now in control.

Lessons[1]

1. **Trusts are tools commonly used in estate planning.** They can be found in wills and can come into existence during your life or at death.

2. **The two types of trust generally used are revocable, which can be changed or even terminated during your life, and irrevocable, which are permanent.**

---

1 These Lessons on Trusts are intended as a cursory overview. They are not intended as legal advice and professional counsel should be consulted in any legal planning.

3. **While trusts have myriad purposes, typically they are used to establish rules under which legal and financial business is conducted.**

4. **Generally, a trust can perform the same functions as an individual.** It can buy and sell property, hold and make investments, operate a business or provide support to a beneficiary.

5. **A trust must be funded in order to operate.** It receives transfers or gifts that provide the means to perform instructions established by the donor or grantor. Without the gift or transfer of a tangible asset, a trust is just an empty shell. It can only control what it possesses, that is, what was been put into it.

6. **Once an asset is transferred into an irrevocable trust, it no longer belongs to the donor/grantor and if drafted properly, is not includable in his estate.**

7. **Since transfers into revocable trusts can be changed, they do not qualify as completed gifts and so they remain legally yours.**

8. **Historically, the largest tax that can be imposed is the estate tax.** Since it is such a large revenue producer, it's likely to continue in some form.

9. **It's important to fully understand how a trust functions and whether you need one before moving forward.**

10. **Always get competent legal help when considering trusts.**

"Everything in life is most fundamentally a gift. And you receive it best when you hold it with very open hands."

Leo O'Donovan

Chapter 10

TO BE OR NOT TO BE?

Elizabeth had just lost her husband of fifty years. She looked much grayer than when I last saw her. She was emotionally beaten, her spirit subdued. Her son Randy didn't know what to do. How do you ease your parent's pain of losing a lifetime partner? How do you calmly talk about money as though he was not dead and you would still see him when you went home to an empty house? Obviously nervous, Randy joked too much and laughed too loud. Occasionally, Elizabeth would display a spark of cognizance. She would emerge from her shell and be back in the room with us again. Her attorney commented that all of the planning had worked as intended. Everything would go where it was supposed to go. Any taxes paid would be minimal. At that point I wondered if any of this made any difference. It certainly didn't seem important to Elizabeth.

Comment

We plan our final affairs for those we love, not for ourselves. Whether rich or poor, we have equal portions of love to bestow. The monetary and spiritual gifts we leave behind demonstrate that love and continued presence after our death. It's the only way we can reach out and touch future generations or a chosen charity. We can still be there for our family when they need us, reinforcing the lessons we taught and the plans we made while still alive. Done correctly, we all can be there for our families after we have died.

Discussion

Documenting one's last wishes is probably not high on anyone's bucket list. I admit that I agonize over the revisions needed for my own estate documents. At this point, it's almost a joke between my attorney and me. While my initial documents primarily addressed taxes and guardianship of our children, life has raced past their relevance. The trust for my children — cleverly crafted to give them half their money at age 25 and the rest at age 30 — is now fodder for the shredder. The point here is that life does not stand still and neither should your planning.

There is an important reason we go through the process of creating wills and trusts. **If we don't specify what should occur, someone else will do it for us.** The great misconception is that some family-friendly entity within the court system will magically bestow the best possible options for those we leave behind. The truth is that without your valid written legal instructions, events will unfold according to the prevalent law of the state where you reside. Things may be completely different than you intended. If the deceased were able see what was to occur, it might cause their death all over again.

Most people recognize the need for a last will but not everyone understands what a will can do. A will defines the distribution of our estate, the primary job of our executer. A will can also create trusts, permanent entities that can continue the execution of our desires for years after our deaths. As mentioned previously, we can create structures that will manage assets, provide for the health, welfare and education of our loved ones, make charitable gifts and minimize the effect of estate and inheritance taxes. If we effectively use the many estate-planning tools available to us, we can keep most of what we have accumulated throughout our lives and influence how it will be spent or maintained.

We may be aware of the need to create a trust for our children in our wills, but we tend to think of doing so only when they are minors. In fact, we can create entities that will provide for them throughout their lives without ever giving them full access to the funds. My trust attempted to provide a failsafe for children who might not be mature enough to inherit the full value of my estate. Suspecting that they might gain wisdom with age or after squandering the first half of their inheritance, I delayed having them receive the estate's second portion by five years. Of course, you can impose rules as varied as your children. The same can be done for a spouse who may not be the best manager of money or budget. However, should you try to place assets away from your spouse, be aware that many states have a provision that will not allow you to fully disinherit a spouse. In any case, give some serious thought as to how you wish the beneficiaries of your estate to receive their inheritance. Keep in mind that as long as you are alive, you can always change your mind.

Another useful estate planning tool is the testamentary trust, which can be written while we are alive but doesn't spring to life until after our death through the direction of our will. Creating any trust requires administration, funding with assets and in some cases, giving things away forever. A testamentary trust allows us to consider what might happen after our deaths from both a human perspective and a tax standpoint, and include something in our will to handle the situation. For example, our will could create a trust for a disabled child unable to support himself. The trust would provide funds for life without disqualifying him from outside assistance. A testamentary trust could create a separate trust designed to receive just enough of our funds to avoid a state inheritance tax or federal estate tax. So not only are we are not paying taxes, our loved ones can have access to the income from the trust. A trust in our will can also provide tuition for our children and grandchildren and, if they don't use all the money, our great grandchildren. If there are several people we wish to help after our deaths, we can have the trustee treat them all equally, discriminate or use his own best judgment to determine who needs the most help. Creating a properly planned trust and choosing a competent trustee can serve as an extension of ourselves after we are gone.

While nothing can replace the loss of a loved one, good planning helps us feel that everything was done as well as possible. We may never get over our awkwardness in expressing grief but we can look at the living and appreciate the life and love they represent. We can take pleasure in the accomplishments of our children and grandchildren. We should cherish the time we are given and be grateful for what we have to give back, however great or little it may be. I will be sure to call my attorney tomorrow.

Lessons

1. **Planning your estate is not only about taxes: It's your opportunity to direct things after your death.** You may provide for family, donate to charity or provide educational help, as well as many other things you might have done while alive.

2. **Just as we age and change, so do our families and circumstances.** Review your estate documents regularly to keep up with the changing needs of your family.

3. **Lacking the proper estate planning documents, your estate will default into whatever distribution system is legally mandated**

where you live. If you don't decide what should happen to your estate through proper legal documents, someone else will.

4. **Your will can accomplish a multitude of functions, limited only by your creativity and prevailing law.**

5. **Your will and trusts can be an extension of your directives after death.** You can be an effective contributor to your family even after you are gone.

6. **While a trust is its own entity, a will merely expresses your directives.** Putting a trust into a will gives you an opportunity to create entities that will only come into existence after your death.

7. **A competent estate planning attorney can be an invaluable member of your financial planning team.**

"By the time you are 80 years old you have learned everything. You only have to remember it!"

George Burns

Chapter 11

IT'S ALL IN THE FINE PRINT

The phone call came from California. It was Holly. She wanted to know the beneficiary of her mother's annuity, worth more than $180,000. Shortly after, she called again to ask when the beneficiary designation had been changed from being distributed equally among the three children to solely to her sister Sally. Meanwhile here in New York, her sister Sally had just been in to pick up the forms to surrender the annuity and receive the proceeds. I let her know that she would be responsible to pay taxes when she received the money, and since it was so close to the end of the year, she might wish to wait until January to take the money, thereby pushing the taxes into the following year. She also had a child in college receiving financial aid and the annuity's added income would definitely affect it. I asked if she planned to share the funds with her siblings. Her answer was no.

Holly called again to ask if her mother changed the beneficiary form or if it was done by her sister, using her power of attorney. I suspect Sally will not wait to get the money until next year; she will want to get the proceeds as fast as she can. I am waiting for the call from Holly's attorney.

Comment

When is a person no longer competent to make financial decisions? What is the last date someone should be permitted to change his or her will or remove a beneficiary? While there is little we can do about our short-term memory diminishing in our later years, barring some cognitive impairment, our long-term memory should serve us well throughout our lives. When then is the final date someone should be able to disinherit their loved ones? Who is competent to attest to that date? Does an argument with a child erase a lifetime of love and care? We will likely encounter and struggle with our own emotional and mental difficulties in later life. What checks and balances will we have in place to prevent us from making an irrational decision, one we would never have made were it not for our deteriorated mental state? Of course, we can always depend on our children to do the right thing. After all, they are family, aren't they?

Discussion

I suppose it's true that a dysfunctional family will end in a dysfunctional state of final affairs. Perhaps it's also true that we reap what we sow. This seems particularly apparent when money enters the fray. The good thing about a will is that you can change it as long as you are alive and no one is questioning your mental competency. The bad thing is that you may be incompetent and not know it. You may die having done something you would have regretted had you really understood. The distribution of your estate is driven by the choices you make during your life. The beneficiary designations on your annuities, IRA, life insurance and even Transfer on Death accounts send the money directly to where it is supposed to go. Whoever's name you placed on the form is going to be the recipient of the proceeds. The institutions holding the funds do not care and cannot become involved in what should have happened, yet alone what is good and right. They will execute their duty to the letter of their contract.

Many people live under the misconception that their will alone is the final disposer of their estate. They believe that their trusted executor, usually the favorite or brightest child, will understand their wishes and act accordingly. The truth is that the executor's responsibility is to pay the bills and distribute the estate according to the will.

What if nothing goes through your will? How will your final expenses be paid? Who pays your mortgage if all the money passes outside the will? How do Holly and her brother get their fair share of mom's will if all of the money was in the annuity that went to Sally? Obviously, they don't! The funds flow as indicated by the contractual agreements and beneficiary designations. The executor could be left with nothing to distribute. Holly and her brother are out of luck. This, of course, leads to some nasty phone calls, correspondence and finally, legal action. After fruitlessly spending lots of money on legal fees, the letter of the law or contract will be carried out. In the interim, accusations will be exchanged as to when mom did what.

While you can protect yourself from inadvertently disinheriting your spouse or children, it's rare that anyone actually does a decent job of organizing their financial affairs. Even if some thought has been put into the flow of one's assets after death, the forms necessary to correct any errors are often left unsigned in the safe deposit box. Lacking signatures, those forms are not worth the paper they are written on. Only properly verified and executed documents have any meaning. In this regard, you typically get what you paid for. If you have paid nothing to have your affairs put professionally in order, you probably will get an equal benefit.

Consider a legacy in which you inadvertently pit your children against each other because of misunderstanding, misinformation or manipulation. While your intention may have been to treat them equally, the reality is that some may get everything while others get nothing. This may sound improbable but I have seen numerous instances where the transfer of assets from one invest-ment to another, or from firm to firm, failed to carry the intended registration and beneficiary designation. A child living close to the parent may have been placed on an account for convenience. If the registration of that account is left unchanged and the parent dies, the funds in that account may go solely to that child. This may not have been the intention of the parent.

All too often, confusion and poor organization of financial af-fairs spawn opportunities for mistakes and manipulation. While there are numerous laws and agencies to protect elder citizens from deceptive schemes, nothing protects them from their chil-dren. Knowing that mom is going to die soon, the child's financial interest may become a driving factor in the arrangement of the parent's assets, whether consciously or not. Simply changing — or failing to change — a beneficiary can completely disrupt an other-wise sound estate plan. As the parent becomes psychologically and emotionally dependent, the child takes control of the assets and affairs, and the opportunity for self-directing the funds arises. In a confused state and grateful to the caregiving child, the parent may even reward the child with assets diverted from siblings. Who is to say whether this is right or fair? After all, it is the parent's money.

Clearly, there are few things uglier than a family fighting over mom's money. With the intrusion of spouses, in-laws and other quasi-related family members, individuals quickly become indig-nant, jealous and self-righteous. A lifetime of love may be unable to withstand the allure of a pile of money, even a small one.

Lessons

1. **Your last will and testament will direct the disposition of your assets after death.** It can be flexible and contain various means of holding or distributing funds to others, directly or indirectly, as you desire. However, it has no control of assets that will not pass through it.

2. **Beneficiary designations on IRA accounts, annuities, and life insurance policies will direct the funds to those you designate.** These assets will not pass through your will unless you have indicated that your will or estate should be the beneficiary. Since these assets do not go through a will, there is no probate process and the transaction is private rather than public record.

3. **Contingent beneficiaries can be established for most accounts with beneficiary designations.** Using a contingent beneficiary, you can direct proceeds to secondary persons in the event the first or primary beneficiary has died. You can ensure that proceeds follow a bloodline or per stirpe. Funds intended for your child can go to the children of your children.

4. **Annuities can be used for tax-qualified investments, such as IRAs, or for regular investment accounts.** When used for the latter, earnings taxation is deferred until withdrawal, at which time the beneficiary is responsible for the taxes. The gain on the contract is considered ordinary income in the reporting year after receiving the funds.

5. **Persons holding a durable power of attorney can act financially as if they were the grantor.** They can change beneficiaries, ownership, make buy and sell decisions as indicated in the document.

A durable power of attorney remains in effect even if the grantor becomes mentally incompetent.

6. **It can be very difficult to determine the mental competence of a parent.** That competence or lack of it may create family divisiveness if ownership, titling or beneficiaries are changed.

7. **When are mom or dad not capable of making decisions?** Unless legally challenged, the instructions of the owner of an asset will be carried out.

8. **When the desires indicated by a will are in conflict with the registration and ownership of the assets, the estate plan can become hamstrung.**

9. **All estate planning documents, life insurance policies, and any other instruments having beneficiary designations available should be reviewed periodically to ensure they are correctly titled.**

10. **Receiving money as a beneficiary may have unintended effects.** For example, the addition of ordinary income from annuity proceeds will trigger additional income tax and may affect college financial aid. Annuity settlement options often provide alternatives that may be desirable, given the beneficiaries' specific financial situation.

Chapter 12

IT'S ABOUT THE MONEY STUPID

The phone call was not pleasant. The market was in a steep decline, and Ella wanted to know the value of the account today. Was there something wrong? How could it have gone down from $180,000 last year when her mother died to just $120,000 today? Good questions but with unpleasant answers. Disbelieving what she was told, Ella's husband was soon on the phone trying to get a different answer. There was nothing I could do. They had controlled the account since the death. Yes, the value was greater a year ago; the death benefit payable from the annuity was $180,000 at the time. Yes, it had now adjusted to reflect the current market value, $120,000. What happened? The couple failed to submit the death benefit forms to the insurance company last year. Why? A court order obtained by an irate brother stopped them. As a result, the account had lost approximately one-third of its original value. No, there is nothing anyone can do until the legal matter is settled.

Comment

It's a little known fact that at death, investments owned by the deceased are often frozen and changes are not allowed. Legally, once the owner dies, there is no one left to give instructions. Until the new legal owners of the account are determined, it's like a drifting ship without a captain to steer it. If invested in the stock market, it will rise and fall in response to the market.

Logic suggests that it might be wise to move everything to cash or a money market when someone dies, but logic has nothing to do with the legal obligations of those involved. Without the owner's instructions, no changes can be made. As such, it usually makes sense to distribute the assets as soon as possible or at least set up an estate account that someone can manage. Family quarrels about beneficiaries or disposition expose the assets to changes in value due to external market fluctuations.

Discussion

Ella's situation is tragic but all too common. Nothing creates family rifts faster or greater than greed. Brothers and sisters who have spent lives together in loving and caring relationships end up with subpoenas and Show Cause orders. It's ironic that while a parent's poor health typically results in help and care from one or more of the children, the death and availability of money gets the attention of all. Greed has caused siblings to become estranged, cousins separated and families torn asunder. When confronted, everyone will be quick to say it's not about the money, but of course, it is! The same denial that naturally occurs when we are forced to recognize the mortality of our parents provides us with our own natural defense. We are able to stow our selfishness and greed into a neat compartment. We believe we are entitled, that our parents would have wanted us to do this even if it is contrary to their written instructions.

Disposing of assets like life insurance policies, annuities, IRA accounts and jointly titled assets can be easily handled. There's little to dispute. Their contractual language and direction determine what to do with the money. If beneficiaries exist, they get the funds. In situations with joint assets, the property is divided if held in tenants in common or passed on in entirety if with rights of survivorship. Money can be passed per capita, as per ownership interest or per stirpes, through the bloodline of the owners. Despite all the tools available to properly title assets, people seldom take full advantage of the opportunity. With proper planning, the vast majority can avoid questions about disposition of assets or be subjected to the probate process. Clearly, understanding how things are disposed of after our deaths goes a long way in preventing undo legal difficulties and emotional family stress. Of course, even with the proper planning, titling and legal instruction, nothing will stand in the way of a disinherited child who feels that he or she has been cheated.

Transferring assets should not be a problem for most widows, widowers or beneficiaries. If the various investments are titled properly and the beneficiaries are in order, it's usually just a matter of obtaining death certificates, notifying the various entities holding the assets and providing forms. Typically, some legal documentation is necessary. Simply put, before things can be transferred, some proof need exist that the funds are going to the right person, that the person doing the transferring has the authority to do so and that no lien is due to creditors or governments. An attorney can be helpful, even with small estates, to help sort through legal requirements.

As mentioned previously, contractual assets such as life insurance, annuities, IRAs and 401(k) plans avoid the probate process if an individual beneficiary is named. The funds go directly where intended with the provision of a death certificate. The funeral home often submits the life insurance death claim for quick payment of final expenses. Often, instead of a check, a money market account is provided, one offering nominal interest that can be accessed immediately. The financial planner or agent usually retains larger life insurance policies and processes the claim.

Investment accounts, individual stocks or bonds are a bit more difficult. In most states, it's possible to establish a ***Transfer on Death*** registration for an investment account, which acts the same as naming beneficiaries. The funds go to the named beneficiaries, avoiding the will and probate process. It becomes more difficult if the individual securities, stocks and bonds are not held by a brokerage firm in an investment account…their existence may be unknown. If held by a transfer agent, or if the client holds the actual certificates, it can be some time before they are found. Then, they must be deposited somewhere before they can be transferred to a new owner. This requires opening a new account in the name of the estate of the deceased and depositing the certificates. If the deceased owned stock for a long time it may have split several times. It also may be worthless.

It's not unusual to receive a letter containing a dividend check made out to someone who died months ago. While usually smaller amounts, processing the transfer of these assets can be extremely difficult. Another processing nightmare is the estate containing securities that have not been properly accounted for through multiple generations. It's not uncommon for someone to inherit a "family" portfolio established long ago that has been transferred by both gift and inheritance with multiple owners. It's quite possible that each of the separate current owners will have a different cost basis, making it exceptionally difficult to determine the taxes when the assets are sold.

Obtaining a new registration for the securities may be almost impossible, since the transferor must have the legal right to transfer ownership to a new person. Consider a stock owned jointly by a couple that die years apart. Upon the second death, in order to get the stock to the new beneficiary, previous ownership must be cleaned up. Needless to say, over time, documents may be lost and events forgotten. Recreating or even remembering what happened is seldom an easy task but necessary in order to transfer the stock.

In planning, I believe asset ownership and beneficiary designation is as important as asset allocation. Half the planning battle is gaining a solid understanding of how things are transferred and taxed. In my experience, more disputes arise over who is getting the money than how much money is at stake. In Ella's situation, settling a legal dispute in court subjected her investment to a stock market decline. Had she and her brother worked out their dispute ahead of time, both would have been wealthier and happier. Of course, I may be wrong. After all, it is all about the money, stupid!

Lessons

1. **The owner's death may cause an investment account to be frozen and no changes can be made until new ownership is established.**

2. **While investment accounts are frozen, the assets remain invested according to the last instructions of the deceased owner.**

3. **The market value of frozen accounts will generally fluctuate with the increase or decrease of the underlying investments.**

4. **Brokerage firms, insurance companies and other entities holding securities for individuals generally will not transfer assets unless clear title to the assets is demonstrated.** In the event of a legal dispute, assets will be held in the name of the deceased, "as is," until the dispute is legally satisfied.

5. **Assets are typically transferred by contract or through a will.** Contracts typically have a beneficiary designation so the assets go directly to the beneficiary. Assets passing through a will undergo a legal process during which the will is determined valid, the executor is appointed, creditors are sought out, taxes are paid and the assets ultimately distributed.

6. **Transferring the assets of a deceased should not be difficult, assuming proper titles and beneficiaries.**

7. **In many states, investments accounts now carry Transfer on Death registration, facilitating the transfer and avoiding the probate process.**

8. **Holding securities in a brokerage account can be helpful in transferring assets since they are transparent, priced daily, shares adjusted for splits or redemptions, and the cost basis easily recorded.** Transfers and/or sales can be quickly accomplished.

9. **Assets held by individuals and kept personally may be lost, forgotten, or even unknown at the time of their death.**

10. **In accounts with multiple owners, the cost basis of the assets may be different for the various owners.** Currently, many assets receive an increase in cost basis, or step up, at death while assets received as gifts retain the cost basis of the previous owner.

"All human plans are subject to ruthless revisions by Nature, or Fate, or whatever one prefers to call the powers behind the Universe."

2010: Odyssey Two

Arthur C. Clarke

Chapter 13

IN OUR MOUNTAIN HIDEAWAY

The kids all wanted mom and dad to retire to the lake. *The family had spent many happy days there and even members of the extended family loved vacations in the family's former homestead. For generations, they lived and played along the placid shores, enjoying the clear water. True, the old house was gone. The cost of new property had skyrocketed just as it had anywhere close to water. The folks had worked hard and now, in their retirement, were going to live the rest of their lives as it was always intended; they deserved it! It would be great for the kids and grandkids too, another reason to build a big new home by the water that everyone could enjoy. Sure, the payments could be an issue but Jerry's pension and social security should make it doable. He and Kathy might even tap some of the other modest assets they accumulated while he was teaching.*

Everyone assumed it would work out okay. Halfway through construction, however, Jerry had a stroke. He would never recover but he would also not die quickly. Kathy couldn't even get the once-strapping man in or out of his wheelchair without help. Meanwhile, construction continued as the couple's assets began to dwindle.

Comment

If we plan properly during our working years, our retirement's greatest risk will be our health. The elephant in the room is proper planning. Without realistic assumptions about your income, both direct (which comes from pensions and social security) and indirect (which is generated from your assets), a plan is as worthless as the paper it's printed on. Once retired, you are unlikely to accumulate additional assets unless through inheritance. Since you are no longer working, your earned income stream has been turned off. What you can spend is what you already have. You are unlikely to suddenly discover how to outperform the market averages in retirement. Further, those averages are just that; averages. Stocks and bonds rarely produce consistent returns. They fluctuate in value and if you are forced to sell something at the wrong time, the averages are irrelevant because you will lose money. Unrealistic assumptions about investment returns only amplify retirement money problems.

Discussion

Everyone has a different vision for retirement. Some want to live on the beach; others up in the mountains; some want to just stay put. We all wish for financial comfort. No one plans to retire and struggle.

Being on a fixed income means just that: it's fixed. While you may enjoy small increases through cost of living adjustments or investment performance, you must live within your means. Therefore, you must understand your means. Where will your income come from? How much will your expenses increase over time? Will the former always be adequate to pay the latter? Is your income dependent on your spouse? Will a premature death cause a dramatic change in income? Have you adequately planned for the increased and uncovered cost of medical care as you age?

While you can agonize over retirement figures and projections, the analysis can be very simple: what you have is what you've got! At retirement, you can easily calculate how much income will come in monthly and how much will need to be spent. If the two don't match, you have a problem. If they do and there is some surplus, you can breathe easier. What you can't do is fantasize that somehow things will be better than what you know to be reality. If you have crunched the numbers and it looks as though you will be short during retirement, you have three choices:

⇨ Keep working until you have enough to retire.

⇨ Reduce expenses and live within your means.

⇨ Take your chances.

If you are going to embark into retirement using optimistic projections, you should begin with an inventory of your assets and income, expenses and liabilities. If we define risk as the uncertainty of an asset's market value on a specific day, you should separate your assets and income between those with market risk and those having none. Income generated from non-fluctuating assets (pensions, social security and assets uncorrelated to the stock market) should be used for fixed and non-discretionary expenses. In other words, use the income and assets you can depend upon to pay the bills you know are necessary. For other discretionary expenses, allocate income and assets from the remaining balance. Now review your lists. It should be clear whether or not you have enough income from your assets to pay essential expenses. If not, you need to find a solution. While this assessment may seem like a simple exercise, it's the first step toward more complex calculations that will reveal how you might fare in retirement.

In the case of Jerry and Kathy, it should have been clear from the beginning that their income and assets were at best marginal to support a mortgage for an expensive home in a rising property tax area. However, the wishes of the parents, combined with the hopes of the adult children, were enough to convince them that building an expensive new home was a good idea. Everyone had unrealistic expectations or at least a profound ignorance of reality. No one anticipated Jerry's health being a factor in the equation but, as in most situations, it is the unplanned that causes the most problems. The extreme cost of home health care (in this case supported by under the table payments to a caregiver) was sufficient to deplete the modest investments the couple had accumulated. His lingering existence cost them more than $60,000 a year, money they didn't have and couldn't afford. Jerry's premature death would eradicate the couple's largest income stream — his pension based on 35 years of teaching. Kathy was left without a good solution. The end result is an emotionally and financially distraught widow.

Many people have the false assumption that their home is an investment. It is not and to presume so is to invite disaster. In addition to being where the heart is, a home is the shelter we all covet and represents the standard of living we have come to expect. It's unlikely any of us would sell our homes and willingly diminish our quality of life. We all hope to continue living through retirement with the same physical and financial comfort we enjoyed throughout our lives. Typically, a reasonable objective is to retire in the mortgage-free home of our dreams. We should note that mortgage-free is significant to someone about to end a lifetime of earning income. It's hardly an appropriate time to take on new, large debt.

In Kathy's case, you might speculate she could sell the house and replace some of her lost income. There are several obstacles, however. As of this writing, the bottom has dropped out of the real estate market. Unfortunately, the property tax system is slow to recognize this and may never reduce the taxable value of her home. Even if the house can be sold, where does Kathy live? Her home is where she lives, not an investment property. Converting a home's equity into income producing assets seldom produces a gain in net worth; rent is merely substituted for the cost of home maintenance. The amount of assets remains the same.

Typically, the equity from the sale is needed to pay the new rent or mortgage expense. In effect, assets have merely been shifted from one line on her personal balance sheet to another. If Kathy decides to amortize (spend both the principal and interest from the sale proceeds), her cash flow shortfalls will be fixed for a finite period of time. She will eventually run out of money. The fundamentals will always apply: we must live within our means or know when we are going to die.

Perhaps you noticed that I didn't offer any solutions to Kathy's dilemma. That's because I don't see any. Kathy may eventually have to sell the mountain hideaway because she simply can't afford to keep it. Her income will be greatly reduced, whether Jerry dies or not as her assets will be completely spent providing around the clock care or nursing home care. Regardless of the outcome, she will have to live on her social security as Jerry's pension ends with no survivor benefits. While she may eventually qualify him for Medicaid and keep her home, which is exempt as long as she lives there, her inability to keep up the payments could force the sale. Any proceeds she receives from selling the house will have to be spent down before he can qualify for Medicaid benefits. She can transfer the house to the kids but as we have learned, he will be disqualified from Medicaid for many months depending on the amount of the proceeds.

While there were many errors in planning for this couple, the first was Jerry's failure to provide a pension survivor benefit. He had a choice: take all he could for the rest of his life, or take a bit less and have his pension extend over the life of his spouse as well. The second glaring mistake, of course, was building a house they couldn't afford. I suspect someone may have done projections showing the couple could afford the new home, albeit just barely. I also suspect his income was assumed to be a guaranteed source. At this point, I hope you have concluded otherwise, that is, you should plan for the worst and hope for better.

Lessons

1. **Financial projections are only as good as the input and assumptions made.** No matter how sophisticated the financial planning process, garbage in still equals garbage out.

2. **You must anticipate or at least consider the events that can negatively affect your financial planning.** Ignoring the risk and cost of uncovered health care items is a sure way to disaster.

3. **Actual investor experience is often very different from historical investment returns.** Using an investment's average annual return for planning purposes can be misleading as investors rarely receive the identical results. The timing of purchases and sales and investor behavior cause investor returns to differ from returns of the investment.

4. **Income guarantees are important in retirement planning.** Being able to pass the risk of loss to another entity carries a great deal of weight in determining how to structure income. Pension payments do away with the opportunity of a lump sum settlement, but also remove investment risk and form a solid core from which to build a retirement distribution plan.

5. **Many pensions have survivor benefits options available prior to retirement.** Electing a survivor option constitutes a risk-free

guarantee of continued income for a spouse. The absence of a survivor benefit places a spouse at risk in the event of the premature death of the retiree, whose pension will be reduced or ended, depending upon the election that was made.

6. **Completing retirement projections for a retiree is no different than completing a business cash flow projection.** Income, sources of income and expenses, both essential and discretionary, must be identified.

7. **Planning for a successful retirement is best done by an objective third person.** There's no place for emotional decisions in a reality based on the ability to pay increasing future bills.

8. **Retiring debt free is a worthy goal.** Most people can live comfortably on much less income post-retirement than pre-retirement if they are debt-free.

9. **Selling your primary residence is generally not a good financial planning strategy.** While the value of your home has likely grown over time, so has the value of other, similar properties. It's a *Catch 22* — selling your home may release a great deal of equity but replacing it with another will leave you back where you started. Downsizing or renting may provide a solution if you are willing to change your lifestyle.

10. **The home is generally an exempt resource in Medicaid planning so long as someone (you, your spouse or a dependent child) continues to live there.** In some areas, that home may be brought back into the equation when it is no longer occupied or if there is no expectation that anyone will ever return to it.

"Life is what happens to you while you are busy making other plans."

John Lennon

Chapter 14
GETTING IT RIGHT

Melody died unexpectedly. Not everyone does. *Most of us pass into the hereafter having kicked and screamed ourselves into final acceptance of our fate. Melody's demise was similar to most middle-age women. It wasn't her time. Her children were now young adults, her husband anticipated an early retirement; it wasn't supposed to end like this. She was supposed to hold grandchildren, travel and finally get to live for herself. But that wasn't to be as cancer overwhelmed her. Roger called with the news. We would have to get things in order, file a death claim for the life insurance, separate assets and put them in his name. We would roll over her IRA into his and name the children as new beneficiaries.*

Roger had another surprise for me. He also had cancer and his prognosis was terminal. We would be doing all of this work again within two years.

Comment

No amount of planning can substitute for living experience. While we live we can correct our mistakes. We can anticipate a future and make changes. We can act, react, learn and develop. Each mistake helps us become a better person. Nothing is irrevocable as there is always a tomorrow.

Not so with death, which brings permanence. What you see is what you get. It's too late to correct mistakes we wish we hadn't made. It's too late to rewrite documents that were ignored for too long. There is no opportunity to express what should have been as opposed to what will occur. Death is finality; not only for us but also for the way we have left our written affairs. There's no place for mistakes.

Discussion

Invariably, people pay too much attention to their investment performance and not enough to what will happen to those investments when they die. While we have little control over the stock market or interest rates, we do have the ability to insure what we have will pass or transfer appropriately to those we love. We also can insure that those assets do so with the least difficulty, taxes or publicity possible. All that is required is an understanding of how things are treated upon death and positive action to put things in the order and title we desire. Having said that, it's amazing how little attention is paid to this most basic planning.

Everyone should have a will, but for many their will has nothing to do with who will get their money. A will determines the disposition of assets not already going elsewhere because of the way they are titled, owned, or due to the election of a beneficiary for the account.

Typically, a 401(k) is the largest asset for most individuals. At death, the proceeds of a 401(k) go not through one's will, but to whoever is listed as the beneficiary. The same is true for IRA accounts, 403(b) accounts, life insurance policies, 457 plans or other deferred compensation arrangements, and any other type of account that has a beneficiary. These assets tend to comprise the bulk of what we accumulate during our lives and for many people, all the energy they expend thinking about who gets what in their will could be for naught. For all the time and money invested in planning things through our will, we could have accomplished the same result by simply changing or naming a beneficiary in a document.

While considering beneficiary designations, when is the last time you took a moment to look at yours? How about this for a cruel blow? What if you forgot to change the beneficiary on your life insurance policies from your first spouse to your current and you die? Obviously, you won't know it. At that point, you're dead. But what about your second spouse? What about the children you had together and, certainly, new joint debt? I doubt your first spouse is going to offer any of the proceeds to your second, or be concerned about the mortgage payment that can no longer be met. Does this sound like an absurd situation? It's not. In fact, it's quite common to find the wrong person listed as the beneficiary on a pension, IRA or life insurance policy, even in situations where the correct person is named on a new will. Again, the will has no say over where the money goes.

The way assets are titled or owned has precedence over a will in directing them to people at your death. The house you own jointly with your spouse will not pass through your will for disposition. If something is owned with rights of survivorship, it goes directly to that survivor it does not pass Go and does not collect $200. In actuality, while it doesn't collect the $200 for passing Go, it avoids all the costs of probate and is a simple transaction. Assets other than real estate can also be titled to pass directly at death and avoid your will. Investment accounts, CD's, money markets and anything else that can have a legal document of ownership can be owned with other people and bypass your will. At your death, the investment account in joint name with your spouse will go directly to him or her. Never mind that your will names lots of charities and special bequests. If your will doesn't get any of the money it has nothing to give. Your good intentions are worthless. At worst, the stated intentions in your will may set up a legal conflict if what you have said does not match up with what you have done.

Another newer means of passing assets to others outside your will is the transfer on death (TOD) documentation. In many states, it's now possible to direct assets at death while avoiding joint ownership during life. In the typical joint ownership, or tenants in common ownership, the individuals listed on the account are actually owners. If they did not make actual contributions to the account, a gift, equal to the amount of ownership they have in the account, was made. As mentioned previously, such gifting can have an effect on Medicaid planning as well as trigger a gift tax circumstance. **A check issued from a jointly owned account is payable to all of the owners and requires their signatures in order to negotiate it.** These accounts are often established with the intention of helping in the administration or management of the account but the desire was never to actually give up ownership. In using a TOD designation, investment accounts will be transferred directly at death without having given up any ownership rights. The TOD, similar to a beneficiary designation, directs the assets simply and privately to the named designees on the form. Once again, assets will avoid going through your will and bypass the probate process.

It may seem that there is something inherently wrong with a person's assets not going through their will but generally, that's not the case. The more assets that avoid a person's will and the court process of probate, the faster, simpler and more private the disposition of their assets. The problem is that few people keep up with their estate planning. The vast majority incorrectly believes that their wills, however simple they may be, will get money and property to the right people. This is the case only if they have planned correctly and followed through with ownership, TOD and beneficiary designations. If not, things will go where they will go.

Consider the case of Melody and Roger again. They were certainly not rich. Like many people, they accumulated numerous assets, held in different forms throughout their lives. Their IRAs, 401(k)s, life insurance and savings account would pass not just from Melody to Roger, but subsequently and altogether too quickly to their children. In this case, except for the ownership of their home, nothing would pass through their will. The majority of their wealth would transfer to the named beneficiaries and designees as they had intended.

Roger called me for the last time recently. He asked me to deal directly with his son in law, the executor of his will and appointee for his powers of attorney. Roger's struggle with cancer was all he could handle and he knew it was a battle he would not win. He thanked me for everything we had done over the years and said goodbye. While I continue to marvel at his strength in acceptance of death, I respect him more for what we accomplished during his life. I was able to hang up the phone knowing that we had done everything we could, everything we should, and that we had done it right.

Lessons

1. **Estate planning documents, including the will, powers of attorney and beneficiary designations, are the most important pieces of any financial plan.** Unfortunately, they are often neglected to the detriment of all.

2. **Your will directs the distribution of any assets not otherwise directed by a form of ownership or statement of beneficiary.**

3. **A common mistake is assuming that your will has control over assets it does not.** The stated desires in your will may not occur if you failed to provide adequate money to pass through your will.

4. **For the majority of Middle America, the largest asset we own will be directed by something other than our will at our death.**

5. **401(k) plans, IRAs and many investment accounts have mandatory beneficiary designations that will avoid passing through our wills and the probate process.**

6. **Life insurance is often the largest asset in an estate, particularly for younger families.** The insurance beneficiary designation will direct the distribution of the proceeds.

7. **There is no intrinsic benefit or detriment to any of the many ways available to distribute assets at our death.** The determining factors in how things should be structured depend on our individual desires and the form of the assets.

8. **Funds passing through a beneficiary designation or ownership form are generally processed more quickly and privately than things passing through a will and the probate process.**

9. **Most estate planning is flexible; you can always change the documents as your needs change.**

10. **At death, what you have put into place is what will occur whether it is what you wished or not.**

"It is my last wish to be buried sitting up!"

Bette Davis

Chapter 15
SOMETHING TO TALK ABOUT

Ann and Lee were going through their mother's dressers. It had been ten months since Grace died and it was past time to sort out the clothes, memorabilia and treasures she left behind. Together, they agonized through her heart-wrenching death, a yearlong battle with cancer. They supported her through the bad days and rejoiced with her on the good ones. They smiled and laughed together as often as they could. They cried at her bedside when she died.

The two girls did the best they could for Grace's final arrangements. Dad had passed many years before and they could only guess at what Grace would have wanted. The service was beautiful. Throngs of friends and family came to the open casket viewing. The Mass was solemn and she was laid to rest next to her husband in the veteran's cemetery.

At the bottom of a drawer they discovered a box. In it was a letter from their mother to them. It was her final wishes and they had got it all wrong.

Comment

We are not immortal. Inevitably, we all will end up in the same state. We will all die sooner or later, whether naturally or unnaturally. While few of us may openly welcome our demise, at least we will be spared having to make any more decisions. Our worries will be taken away from us. Our choices and decisions will fall to those left behind, who will have the task of providing for us after our death. They will try their best to fulfill our final wishes. With both our final arrangements and final affairs, those involved will do their best to honor our memory and sort out our affairs as we would have wished. Doing these tasks the way we want them done will depend upon what we have told them. They will look to what we have written and what we have said for guidance.

Discussion

While we are reluctant to talk to our families, and often they to us, about final wishes, it is a necessary conversation. Not only must it occur, it must be honest and should be reconfirmed as illness progresses. Why reconfirm? Because who can say with certainty how they will feel about dying and death until actually in its embrace? While I may have strong convictions about final wishes while in good health, I may change my mind when I actually confront death. Hopefully, we will leave this world with the capacity to be cognitive and communicate right up to the end. However, there's no guarantee this will happen. Clearly, there are questions that must be answered.

Some answers are fairly simple and don't require any emotionally-charged discussions:

⇨ Where do you wish to be buried?

⇨ Do you wish to be cremated?

⇨ Where are your important documents and pertinent papers?

⇨ Who are your professional advisors?

⇨ Do you have legal documents in place? Who has them?

⇨ Are there any special requests you would like carried out?

⇨ Is there anything you would really object to?

⇨ Do you wish a religious ceremony?

⇨ Would you prefer a celebration of life?

⇨ Should we have an open casket?

⇨ Are you a veteran? Do you want a military ceremony?

⇨ Do you have a safe deposit box? Who has access?

⇨ Are you an organ donor?

The length of the list will be as long as the person was complicated. It may be short or involve numerous items that reflect the life, beliefs and desires of the deceased.

Some questions are more difficult than others. The survivor may have to decide how the deceased would think, feel or react to certain situations:

⇨ How far should we go in trying to keep you alive?

⇨ Given a choice, would you prefer to forego treatment or have your life extended but with lowered quality?

⇨ If placed on life support how long should it be allowed before it is removed?

⇨ Is there a spouse whose needs or wishes should be considered even if they seem contrary to those of the deceased?

⇨ How do you resolve conflicts that may arise if the deceased had more than one family? It's common to find people who have married more than once and had children from each marriage.

Clearly, whoever is left behind to enact someone's final wishes must try to think and act as the deceased would. How well they perform depends on how well the deceased communicated their wishes prior to death, and how well they chose the person to fulfill that job.

We all know or suspect that having a conversation about final affairs can be uncomfortable at best. The reluctance to talk about these things comes from all parties. Someone mentioned to me recently that it is about growing up. Most often the children, now adults, find themselves facing the mortality of their parents. The parents, now elder, must reluctantly recognize the aged faces in the mirror as their own. The metaphor of stepping into one's parent's shoes becomes very appropriate.

I do not know of any best way to approach this conversation. I only know it needs to occur. In my own experience it was done through humor. One of my sisters-in-law orchestrated an evening complete with wine, snacks and funny jokes. The jokes were interspersed between questions about where to be buried, what type and where would religious services or celebrations be held? It worked with our family. We all ended up laughing as mom and dad found that they didn't agree with each other about several things. The high point came with one of them saying to the other, "What difference does it make to you, you'll be dead?" Unfortunately, one of them did die shortly after this meeting. Thankfully, we already had our meeting, and knew what to do.

I cannot imagine the emotions Ann and Lee experienced upon finding that letter from their mother. Realizing they had done things differently than she would have wanted, did they feel guilt or anger? Did they agonize over missed opportunities to have talked to Grace? Did they wonder if perhaps she had told them and they hadn't listened?

We don't know what circumstances prevented them from knowing about the letter. I do know this was an avoidable situation. Everyone involved had something to talk about. Everyone reading this does as well. Now is as good a time to start as any.

Lessons

1. **We should never be afraid to share thoughts about our final arrangements with family.** As awkward as it may seem, it can done if addressed openly and without emotion.

2. **We leave responsibilities to our survivors for funeral details and for carrying out the wishes in our legal documents.** The clearer we communicate these things, the better.

3. **Be sure to let someone know the location of important legal documents and personal instructions you wish to relay.**

4. **Let someone know if you are an organ donor or have a specific anatomical request.** These decisions should be clearly articulated as early as possible, not made during the latter, emotional phase of dying.

5. **Your final arrangements should be in two parts: the first pertains to the physical arrangements you want, the second to completing your financial affairs.** Ask yourself if you have prepared the proper documents to ensure these two things occur as you wish.

6. **Your Living Will is extremely important. Be sure there is no controversy or misunderstanding about your wishes to be kept alive by extraordinary means or allowed to die.** Speak with whoever will be involved in that decision and make sure uninvolved family members are aware as well.

7. **This conversation does not have to be solemn or morbid, nor have anything to do with illness or disability.** The best time to have it is when everyone is healthy and happy.

8. **Try injecting some humor into the conversation; it works!**

"Well it's a long, long time,
from May to December
but the days grow short
when you reach September."

September Song
Maxwell Anderson

Chapter 16
FINAL THOUGHTS

The call came from Edith in North Carolina. *Husband Gerry was still receiving Hospice care in their home but their children were naturally worried. Each had separate concerns and was quick to express them whether emotional, financial or physical. Are mom and dad okay financially? The children were scattered throughout four states; wouldn't it be better if the folks move closer to one of them? Who would pay for dad's at-home care? Edith was desperate, not because of Gerry's health issues, which were anticipated, or finances, which were adequate. She didn't know how to handle the kids. While their suggestions were all well intended, they were, in her words, "driving us nuts."*

Comment

Gerry and Edith had prepared well, both financially and legally. They had insurance to help with long term care bills, adequate income and assets to provide for a survivor and no debt. They had a strong support group through their local church. They had a great loving life together and were as prepared as anyone could be for the end. Not that Gerry was going to go without a fight. Neither he nor Edith was someone who would lie down and quietly accept fate. At the same time, they understood that at some point, life must come to an end. Gracious is a word that comes to mind in describing their attitude. Perhaps because they belonged to the "greatest generation," their outlook on life and death was different from younger people. I'm sure their profound religious beliefs brought them happiness, acceptance and contentment, not just at the end of life but always.

Discussion

As of this writing, Gerry continues to beat the odds. During our relationship, they had often thanked me for the help I had given them. I promised Edith I would always be there for them, even though they live hundreds of miles away in another state. My last visit to see them was delightful. Edith prepared a wonderful lunch and we worked out some financial details, validating their insurance benefits and reviewing their wills and beneficiary designations. We discussed transferring some vacation property to one of their sons and whether they could afford to move closer to one of their daughters. Since they had no desire to move until things got worse, we concluded they didn't need to do so. We wrapped up the day at a great local restaurant where they offered to pay the bill since I had incurred the expense of flying down and staying in a hotel. They didn't understand why I insisted on paying. What they really didn't understand is how much I owed them because their example taught me so much. They taught me to live each day to the fullest. They taught that while things may not always go the way you want, do the best you can with whatever you have. They taught me that people are more important than things, and that family is the most important of all.

I will miss Gerry and Edith when they are gone just as I miss other close friends and family that have preceded me. One thing I have learned is that we have no control over our late-life health and death. I suggest that we control what we can how we live each day, how we treat those around us and embrace those closest to us. Someone once said, "Living well is the best legacy."

I hope you leave a long and bountiful legacy.

\#   \#   \#

"Life is too short to wake up with regrets. So love the people who treat you right. Forget about the ones who don't. Believe everything happens for a reason. If you get a second chance, grab it with both hands. If it changes your life, let it.

Nobody said life would be easy, they just promised it would be worth it!"

Harvey MacKay

Life is not a straight line. There is no direct travel from beginning to end. It is a series of curves, intersections, switchbacks, yields, stop signs and exits. There is no map to guide us on our journey. There is only us, learning from those who traveled before, trying to do the best we can with the knowledge we have. Life is precious. Time is fleeting. As hard as it may be at times, do your best to appreciate every mile of road we are given. As Jan, my partner in life has taught me so well, the joy really is in the journey!

Made in the USA
Lexington, KY
07 April 2014